FILM KOREA

Published in 2023 by Welbeck

An imprint of Welbeck Non-Fiction Limited, part of Welbeck Publishing Group.

Offices in: London - 20 Mortimer Street, London W1T 3JW & Sydney - Level 17, 207 Kent St, Sydney NSW 2000 Australia

www.welbeckpublishing.com

ISBN 978 1 80279 633 9

Editor: Conor Kilgallon
Design: Russell Knowles, James Pople
Picture research: Giulia Hetherington
Production: Rachel Burgess

Printed in China

10 9 8 7 6 5 4 3 2 1

FILM KOREA

THE GHIBLIOTHEQUE GUIDE TO THE WORLD
OF KOREAN CINEMA

MICHAEL LEADER & JAKE CUNNINGHAM

WELBECK

TAKE CARE OF MY CAT

고양이를
부탁해

20년 만에 4K 리마스터링

기다렸어,
지금의 '너를'
—
그리웠어,
그때의 '우리'

2001.10.13

배두나 이요원 옥지영 이은실 이은주 ✻ 정재은

2021.10.13

CONTENTS

Opposite: High school reunion. A poster for the
20th anniversary re-release of *Take Care of My Cat.*

INTRODUCTION

There aren't many cultures that can be boiled down to just a letter: a simple prefix that can denote a whole, vibrant world. K-pop, K-drama, K-beauty – the Korean Wave (also known as Hallyu) has engulfed the globe over the last two decades, inspiring fans to fall in love with the nation's music, TV and film. From Baby Shark to BTS, *Squid Game* to *Parasite*, no corner of pop culture has been left untouched.

This is our third book. For our first two, we looked at the work of Studio Ghibli, and then surveyed the whole span of Japanese animation through 30 films. Here, we embrace Korean cinema – to our minds the most exciting film industry in the world right now.

Our approach is that we have picked 30 key feature films from South Korea that span genres and eras, from Golden Age classics to contemporary blockbusters, from festival favourites to intriguing indies, each presenting a potential gateway into the industry's output and history. To make things interesting, we restrict ourselves to one film per filmmaker – which proved to be particularly tricky when many of South Korea's top directors, including Bong Joon-ho, Park Chan-wook, and Lee Chang-dong, have several bangers to their name. Each chapter begins with Michael offering us the context, laying out the backstory behind the film before Jake takes the reins for his review. Everything is then capped off with further recommendations if you want to continue down the same path.

Our goal here is to help kick-start journeys. Maybe you have seen *Parasite* and wonder what all the fuss is about; perhaps you're a veteran of the Asia Extreme generation and still recall your first taste of *Oldboy*'s infamous octopus scene; or you might already consider yourself something of a Korean cinema aficionado. Hopefully there will be something for you here. In the UK, we have only ever been given a limited view of South Korea's film history, and there are so many world-class films and filmmakers to discover.

That's what makes Korean cinema such an exciting industry to explore. In the present day, Korean films are winning awards and enjoying international distribution, but there are many rarely seen classics dating all the way back to the 1950s and 1960s, from directors such as Yu Hyun-mok, Shin Sang-ok and Lee Man-hee. Through the efforts of the Korean Film Archive, the UK's Korean Cultural Centre and their annual London Korean Film Festival, these films are slowly becoming more visible and renowned, deservedly so. When the UK film magazine *Sight and Sound* held their decennial Greatest Films of All Time Poll in 2022, there was only one Korean production in the Top 250 – *Parasite*, of course – but who knows how that will change by 2032?

As an industry, Korean cinema is never one note, and resists easy classification and categorization. The success of Tartan Films' Asia Extreme home video label in the early 2000s might have given the impression that all Korean

Opposite: Zombie-horror *Train to Busan* was a box office smash in Korea and became a cult hit around the world.

Opposite: Heavy weather. Na Hong-jin's beguiling and troubling horror-thriller, *The Wailing.*

films were weird and wild, but that couldn't be further from the truth. Of course, we have our fair share of cult genre films here – from dark thrillers to even darker horror films – but they're rubbing shoulders with romantic comedies, melodramas, popcorn spectacle, and independent gems destined for the arthouse or film festival circuit. Perhaps the strongest and most promising thread through this book is the rise of a new generation of women filmmakers, particularly those who have made their debuts in the last decade with a growing canon of finely detailed domestic dramas, such as Kim Bora (*House of Hummingbird*), Yoon Ga-eun (*The World of Us*) and Yoon Dan-bi (*Moving On*).

There are many theories about why Korean cinema is so beloved internationally. From a film fan's point of view, South Korea is simply home to some of the world's greatest working filmmakers, but it is also a country that still provides what Hollywood and English-language cinema at large has lost in the franchise-dominated blockbuster era: distinctive and well-crafted films that play with form and genre, while never forgetting the fundamentals of what makes cinema compelling; versatile stars with clout and charisma who use their wattage across a wide range of film styles; ambitious and adept filmmakers who drink deep from the well of world cinema while finding

their own voice and vision. With so much of the UK's film culture under threat, South Korea's landscape of film schools, festivals, organizations and magazines makes the country seem like a sanctuary for cinephiles.

Contemporary Korean culture is a product of the nation's turbulent modern history. Over the last century, the country has suffered through Japanese imperial rule, the Korean War, division between North and South, successive authoritarian dictatorships, and a complicated transition towards democracy from 1987 onwards. Director Park Chan-wook, in his introduction to *Sight and Sound*'s special issue on Korean cinema in December 2022, wrote that the social strife of those years, and the freedom of expression that followed after decades of censorship and suppression, is something that can be felt throughout Korean culture. This theme crops up throughout this book, but we are film critics, not academics. To learn more about Korean history and its relation to cinema, there's a further reading section at the end of the book.

But now, back to the films. From *The Housemaid* to *Parasite*, *Train to Busan* to *Burning*, some of the world's finest films made by the brightest talents await you over the next 190+ pages. Thank you for picking up this book. Enjoy your journey through Film Korea!

THE WIDOW

미망인

AGAINST ALL ODDS

Shin-ja lost her husband in the Korean War, and now struggles to make a life for herself and her young daughter through a tangle of benefactors, suitors and lovers.

1955

Director: Park Nam-ok

71 mins

When the Seoul International Women's Film Festival launched in 1997, its opening film was a nod to history: a revival screening of the film considered to be the first directed by a Korean woman, 1955's *The Widow* by Park Nam-ok. While it was ignored at the time and, in fact, now exists only in a form that is incomplete, *The Widow* is a landmark film, and Park's story continues to be an inspiration for filmmakers fighting to make their mark today.

Born in 1923 in Hayang, North Gyeongsang, Park Nam-ok was interested in film, literature and the arts from a young age, but found herself drawn to athletics, competing as a teenager at national level as a shot-putter. As an adult, she worked as a film reviewer and as a continuity girl for films, and it was during the Korean War that she cut her teeth editing newsreels. Then, in 1954, she embarked on the ambitious task of shooting a film of her own. The project was very much a family effort: her husband, a playwright, wrote the screenplay, while financing was provided by her sister (the name of the production company, Jamae Films, comes from the Korean word for *sister*).

However, Park herself shouldered the heaviest load of the production – almost literally, as she directed the film with her infant baby strapped to her back. On top of coordinating the shoot, she also had to contend with unrepentant sexism from all quarters: renting film equipment proved to be a challenge, and recording studios reportedly refused to let her hire their facilities, simply because she was a woman. And once the film was finished, cinemas weren't interested in screening the work: on its April 1955 release, the film was on screen for only four days. *The Widow* was to be Park's only work as director; afterwards she moved into publishing, and later emigrated with her daughter to the United States.

The story didn't quite end there, though. Fast forward to the 1990s, and a new generation of women in the Korean film industry were writing their own history. With the help of the Korean Film Archive, *The Widow* was restored for its special screening at the Seoul International Women's Film Festival in 1997 – albeit with some scenes lacking sound and the end missing. Just over a decade later, the festival introduced the Park Nam-ok award in 2008 to commemorate "the first Korean female filmmaker and to remember her life and the reality of women, women's gaze, and women's desires that she portrayed in her 1955 film". The first winner of the prize was director Yim Soon-rye, who had earlier directed *Keeping the Vision Alive: Women in Korean Filmmaking*, a documentary that pays tribute to Park Nam-ok's pioneering work. By the time of her death in 2017, Park's place in Korean cinema history was assured.

Above left: Reflecting on grief. Lee Min-ja in *The Widow*.

FURTHER VIEWING

In the 1960s, Hong Eun-won became Korea's second female feature filmmaker with a run of films including the social drama *A Woman Judge*, about a woman balancing the demands of her job and her family. Other trailblazing female filmmakers of the period include actress-turned-director Choi Eun-hee (pictured) and Hwang Hye-mi. However, it wasn't until the end of the century, and the turn of the new millennium, that a veritable wave of female filmmakers came to prominence, with the likes of Jeong Jae-eun (*Take Care of My Cat*), Lee Jeong-

hyang (*Art Museum by the Zoo*, *The Way Home*), Yim Soon-rye (*Waikiki Brothers*) and Park Chan-ok (*Jealousy Is My Middle Name*) picking up the torch first lit back in 1955 by Park Nam-ok and *The Widow*.

THE WIDOW – REVIEW

Fittingly, for a film that marks a checkpoint in Korean film history, *The Widow* seems to begin at one. The camera steers past a control officer, a booth with a stop sign, onto a bridge and under a banner bearing the country's name. But the signs are written in English, catering for the influx of post-war Western influence. In the 1950s, Korea was caught at the checkpoint between tradition and modernity, and the film examines the many costs that come with making the crossing.

Park Nam-ok's remarkable film finds Shin-ja, a widow who lost her husband in the Korean War, torn over the different directions her life could take in her quickly changing country. Caught between duty and desire, she finds that her care for her daughter is jeopardized by her relationships with a friend of her late husband's, a handsome stranger and the gossiping, "sassy" women who surround her. With the weight of parenthood quite literally on her back during shooting, Park offers a measured, bravely cold and honest portrayal of the challenges of finding liberation while raising a child, which will surprise modern viewers. There's intense emotion in Shin-ja's bond with her daughter Ju, thanks to raw, piercing performances by Min-ja Lee and the young Seong-ju Lee; but there's equal power in her lackadaisical, almost resentful treatment of her daughter, at one point resulting in a stressful beachside scene that sends memories of *Under the Skin* and *Jaws* shivering up the spine. Crucially, Shin-ja isn't defined just by her parenthood; her romantic exploits hold equal weight, Park finding potency in the glances, interactions and fleeting contact between Shin-ja and the men around her.

Park's skills at crafting and combining striking imagery is a constant throughout *The Widow*. Her work making newsreels seeps into the film. When characters take a car journey, it's an opportunity for a travelogue: the trams, signposts and traffic observed and sonically layered, building up a huge sense of bustling urban development and scale, despite the film's limited locations and budgetary scope. Cross-cutting between sequences, a bold editing technique

Above: Clashing costumes and relationships. Park Nam-ok's film uses clothing to outfit rebellion.

for the time, creates a thrilling cat-and-mouse energy to affairs, while ghostly cross-fades of faces pry open Shin-ja's psychological state. Even simple footsteps hitting tarmac, shot from the waist down, repeated in different locations and with different characters, add to the film's hurried atmosphere, while also suggesting that this drama could be happening to any of the people who walk these streets.

Shin-ja's rewriting of women's expectations is just one aspect of how the film grapples with the tug of war between tradition and change. Westernization trickles into the story, offering both desirability and danger: the untrustworthy Taek dresses in a patterned, loose, open collar shirt, a huge contrast to the layered, long traditional hanbok of Shin-ja, and in a bar, a cowboy hat worn by a patron is symbolically knocked off. Characters utter some lines in English like covert sweet nothings, and even the film's score alludes to the sociopolitical landscape, with the familiar American folk song "I've Been Working on the Railroad" snuck in at one point.

The film is not entirely for or against the developments in the country at the time. The film shows post-war Korea as a country becoming less conservative, but one whose culture was being diluted. In its uneasiness, it is something radical, and it's a tragedy that *The Widow* would be the only work in Park Nam-ok's directorial career.

THE HOUSEMAID

하녀

MEET MR MONSTER

A music teacher hires a young woman to help his pregnant wife with the domestic chores. However, this new arrival in the household starts to have an undue influence over the family.

1960

Director: Kim Ki-young

108 mins

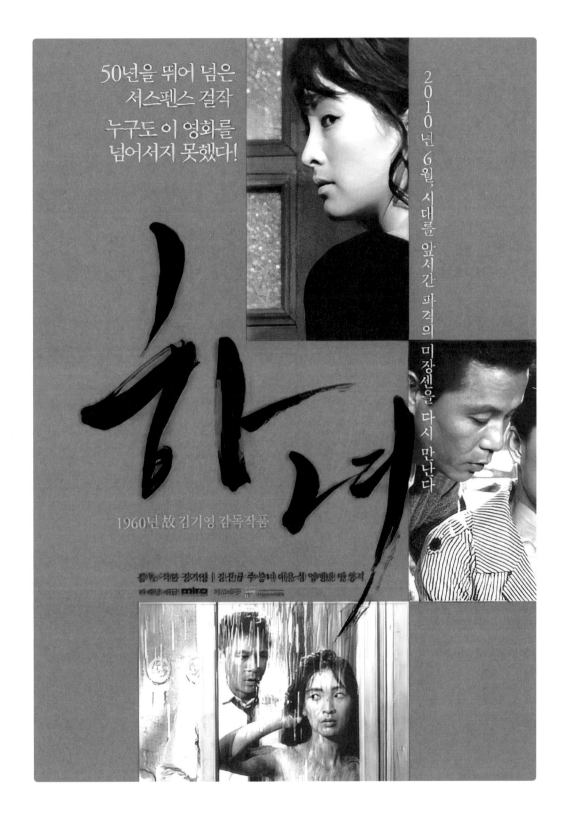

50년을 뛰어 넘은
서스펜스 걸작
누구도 이 영화를
넘어서지 못했다!

2010년 6월, 시대를 앞서간 파격의 미장센을 다시 만난다

1960년 故 김기영 감독작품

Even for committed world cinema fans, the long history of Korean cinema can sometimes be unexplored territory. But if there is one film that has broken through the fog, it is Kim Ki-young's influential 1960 melodrama, *The Housemaid*.

Sources differ about Kim Ki-young's actual birthdate. Official records say 1919, while he himself claimed he was three years younger. Born in Seoul, but brought up in Pyongyang, Kim had his first taste of films aged five, and recalls skipping school to see everything he could. As he put it: "I lived in movies." Later, while studying at Gyeongseong Dental College, he fell in love with theatre, from Ancient Greek plays to the work of Anton Chekhov, William Shakespeare and Eugene O'Neill, and staged a production of Henrik Ibsen's provocative and taboo-breaking play *Ghosts*.

He abandoned a career in medicine, though, when the opportunity arose to make documentaries for the United States Information Service during the Korean War. It was using the skills from these USIS jobs – and borrowing some of the equipment, too – that enabled him to make his early feature films. This post-war era would become known as a golden age for Korean cinema, with Kim placed alongside Shin Sang-ok and Yu Hyun-mok as the period's leading filmmakers. He would soon drift away from his contemporaries, though, into more lurid territory, with 1960's *The Housemaid*

signalling this change in direction. Contemporary reviews bemoaned its "grotesque indulgence", "excessive directing" and "vulgar tastes" – and yet the film was a resounding box office hit.

Kim's career was one of extremes and eccentricity. He twice topped the domestic box office, in 1971 and 1972, with *Woman of Fire* and *The Insect Woman*, but his fiercely independent decision to finance his own films left him facing mounting debts and near bankruptcy, and he was kept afloat only thanks to bailouts from his wife, who had stuck with dentistry. Read into his career, and you'll find all sorts of anecdotes and tall tales, such as him supposedly buying a haunted house because it came with a hefty discount. A fellow director quoted in the booklet essay for the Korean Film Archive's release of *The Housemaid* provides a colourful description of the man: "Director Kim Ki-young is a monster. He is [six-feet] tall, with a big body, dishevelled hair which he has never washed, rough skin that is neither dark nor light, and wide open crayfish eyes, with which he always observes things through a vigilant and anxious expression."

Above: Window of opportunity. Myung-sook spies on the Park family.

Opposite: Smoke gets in your eyes. Part erotic drama, part PSA. *The Housemaid* is a lesson for any potential adulterers.

A true independent and an eccentric, Kim Ki-young eventually fell out of favour, and it seemed that he was destined to be forgotten. In his essay that heralded *The Housemaid*'s landmark release by the Criterion Collection, Kyung Hyun Kim explains that over 70% of films made in the country before 1960 have been lost: cast-off film prints were first used to line the brims of straw hats, while in later years chemists extracted silver from the celluloid film. Several of Kim's films are still lost, or survive only in incomplete prints. In an interview quoted by the Korean Film Council, the director declared, "It's awful to think that nothing remains of the work you gave your whole life to."

It was only through the devotion of a younger generation of budding filmmakers and cult film fans, including the directors Park Chan-wook and Bong Joon-ho, that Kim's work became more widely appreciated and available. A community that had sought out his films on television or VHS, now discussed them on online message boards. This reappraisal hit a peak in 1997, when Kim was the subject of a retrospective at the Busan International Film Festival. Kim was able to experience this rediscovery of his work, but, tragically, he couldn't capitalize on it: in February 1998, he and his wife died in a house fire.

But *The Housemaid* lived on. Retrospectives followed at film festivals around the world, culminating in a restoration of the film in 2008 undertaken by the Korean Film Archive with

support from the World Cinema Project, a film preservation organization founded by Martin Scorsese. "I can safely say [*The Housemaid*] is quite unlike anything I've ever seen," Scorsese says in a filmed introduction for the film. "Personally speaking, I was startled the first time I saw the picture, by its mood of upset, its bold expressionism, its sense of the potential danger in all human interaction, and its intense and passionately realized sense of claustrophobia."

Above: Kim Jin-kyu, who plays Mr Kim, is a dexterous actor. Look out for him in *Aimless Bullet* and *Mother and a Guest*, too.

FURTHER VIEWING

The Housemaid is regarded as a pivotal film in Korean cinema at large, and is integral to the development of the Korean horror genre and its distinctively melodramatic textures. Kim Ki-young would essentially remake *The Housemaid* twice, at 10-year intervals, with 1971's *Woman of Fire* (pictured) and 1982's *Woman of Fire '82*, and further explored the diabolical *femme fatale* character type in 1972's *The Insect Woman* and 1985's *Beasts of Prey* (also known as *Carnivore*). Both Kim and *The Housemaid* have inspired and influenced many younger Korean films and filmmakers over the years, as can be seen in the supernatural horror of *Suddenly in the Dark* (1981), the direct adaptation of Im Sang-soo's *The Housemaid* (2010), the charged thrillers of Park Chan-wook, and Bong Joon-ho's domestic satire *Parasite*.

THE HOUSEMAID – REVIEW

The Housemaid is formally ambitious, emotionally startling and dripping in horror. Before the story even begins, as chilling wind instruments and a bleeding-text title card swoop in, it's clear this isn't a standard melodrama but something far more uneasy. A game of cat's cradle between two children soon follows, the close-up web of flesh and fingers foreshadowing the potentially knotty binds between family innocence and domestic trap which are to follow.

The handsome Mr Kim (just ask all the gossiping women who attend his choir practice) has a wife pregnant with a third child and a dilapidated new house to convert, and looks for a housemaid who can help smooth out his increasingly stressful domestic life. The factory worker Myung-sook takes the role. From her first moments in the house, when she catches a rat with her bare hands and licks her lips when eyeing up some poison, it's clear that Myung-sook's residency will not unfold in the most delightful way.

As Myung-sook burrows deeper into the family life of the Kims, she disturbs their harmony and eventually Mr and Mrs Kim's monogamy. Although extramarital affairs were a hugely controversial act, and still are in today's Korea, director Kim Ki-young skilfully layers a pulsing sexuality through the film, so when Mr Kim bows to fate it seems inevitable. Shared piano lessons, a puff on a cigarette, even the veined, seemingly breathing walls of the house, have a carnality to them. Myung-sook could be a screeching bunny boiler, but Lee Eun-shim's compellingly unpredictable performance makes it so much more, her eyebrows slithering between arch schemer and pursed innocence in a second.

Contained mostly within the walls of the Kim family home, the staging of *The Housemaid* is hugely impressive, taking its quaint setting and warping it into both a cage and a maze. Decorated with insinuating masks, the house is built with wafer-thin sliding doors that hide lust just millimetres away, wide open windows that voyeuristically tantalize – and to connect them, tracking camera movements that peer between the private and public. Perhaps most impactful, though, is

Above: Ju Jeung-ryu and Lee Eun-shim show the black-and-white divide between the purity of the domestic and the devilishness of the disruptor.

the central staircase. Rivalling the Odessa Steps scene from *Battleship Potemkin*, these steps offer dramatic depth of image, with characters looming menacingly away at the top, descending through their desirous actions and meeting shocking ends at the bottom. It's a bridge to violence, infidelity and murder. Watch Park Chan-wook's *Stoker* or Bong Joon-ho's *Parasite*, and you'll see the influence of the Kims' staircase, a passageway to secrets and salaciousness.

As well as its mise-en-scène and storytelling prowess, the editing of *The Housemaid* is another achievement. The sliding doors and camera movements fasten together, maintaining immersion between scenes and keeping viewers locked in the Kim household. Elsewhere, quick, lyrical cuts match together trains, street lights and a lamp bulb, transforming a character's journey home from dull exposition into a striking, but smooth motion, that keeps the attention.

After such an immersive experience, one editorial choice breaks through the sliding fourth wall, in a fascinating and surprising way. Once comeuppances have been dealt, and Chekhov's rat poison has been put to one side, Mr Kim takes a moment to address the viewers. The message is delivered with a wide smile and big laugh as director Kim Ki-Young returns to his roots making information service films, telling us that this story could happen to anyone. Audacious and entertaining, *The Housemaid* might be the most depraved Public Service Announcement ever made.

AIMLESS BULLET
(OBALTAN)

오발탄

THE COST OF LIVING

In the bleak post-war Korean landscape, a beleaguered accountant struggles to support his family, including his pregnant wife, his trauma-stricken mother, his unemployed army veteran brother, and his sister, a former nurse who now works as a prostitute servicing American soldiers.

1961

Director: Yu Hyun-mok

110 mins

A YU HYUNMOK FILM

AIMLESS
BULLET

Hailed as one of the pivotal masterpieces of Korean cinema, *Aimless Bullet* is routinely ranked highly in greatest film lists, often taking the top spot. Critic Kim Jyoun-wook refers to the film's impact and legacy as equivalent to that of *Citizen Kane* in Hollywood history, and credits its director, Yu Hyun-mok, as one of the inventors of modern Korean cinema.

Yu was born in 1925 in Sariwon, in what is now North Korea. His father was a landlord and his mother, a devout Christian, was a shop owner, and Yu enjoyed an affluent upbringing. From a young age, he was a cinemagoer, and recalls sitting on his father's lap and watching the influential silent film *Arirang* (1926), one of the first major homegrown films, which he would remake decades later. However, his career in cinema wasn't inevitable. After finishing high school, he first applied to become a pastor, and then pursued studies in theology, before changing track to study Korean language at Dongguk University in Seoul with a focus on drama. He chalked up the change of heart to seeing *Crime et châtiment* (1935), Pierre Chenal's French-language film adaptation of Fyodor Dostoevsky's *Crime and Punishment*, which he watched at the cinema 14 times.

While studying, he devoured books on montage by Soviet filmmakers Vsevolod Pudovkin and Sergei Eisenstein in his college library, attended lectures in screenwriting at the National Library of Korea and took every opportunity he could to gain on-set experience, eventually working as an assistant director. He graduated from university in 1950, the year that saw the start of the Korean War. As the war divided the country in two, Yu was cut off from his family, and by the end of the war in 1953, he had lost his father and six siblings in the conflict. His mother, who rebuilt her life in Busan, urged her son to pursue his dream of directing. Looking back on those years, Yu told Kim Jyoun-wook that "the tragedies brought upon my family by the war grew sorrow and despair within me", no doubt influencing the weighty themes he wished to explore in his work.

Aimless Bullet, Yu's eighth feature, was adapted from a novella by Yi Beom-seon that the director said captured both the destitution of the post-war period, and a sense of "aimlessness and loss of direction" that pervaded the nation, comparing it to Albert Camus' existentialist work *The Stranger*. Shot on a shoestring budget on the streets of Seoul, the film married the influence of Italian Neorealism ("I was so stupefied on viewing the *Bicycle Thieves*," Yu recalled, "that I fell into a gutter in front of the theatre") with the spiritual qualities of the films of Robert Bresson and Ingmar Bergman. The film was released in April 1961, mere weeks before the military coup d'état of May 16, led by Park Chung-hee. As a result, the release

was suppressed, and returned to cinemas only after it had been screened, and positively reviewed, at the San Francisco International Film Festival in 1963 – a screening that played an important role in the film's enduring legacy. A 35mm subtitled print of the film was the sole surviving complete copy, and served as the source for the Korean Film Archive's digital restoration of *Aimless Bullet* in 2015.

Below: Cherry on top. In a film of many stunning images, this rare romantic moment sparks brightly.

FURTHER VIEWING 👁

Due to his aesthetic, spiritual and sociopolitical ambitions, Yu Hyun-mok often struggled with censors and commercially minded financiers throughout his career, and eventually embarked on a second career as a film professor. Several of his films are now available via the Korean Film Archive's YouTube channel, including the Grand Bell award-winning anti-communist films *Descendants of Cain* (1968) and (one of Yu's favourite films) *Rainy Days* (1979), as well as the social drama *Daughters of Kim's Pharmacy* (1963) and the audacious, avant-garde film *An Empty Dream* (1965). As a producer, Yu found unlikely success in the 1970s with a series of animated features, including the giant-robot sci-fi *Robot Taekwon V* (1976) and the Wonder Woman knock-off, *Fly, Wonder Princess* (1978).

Above: A City of Sadness. *Aimless Bullet*'s urban setting is as much a prison as it is a home.

Below: Set just after the war, Yu Hyun-mok's film sees confused, pained characters searching for emotional and professional connection.

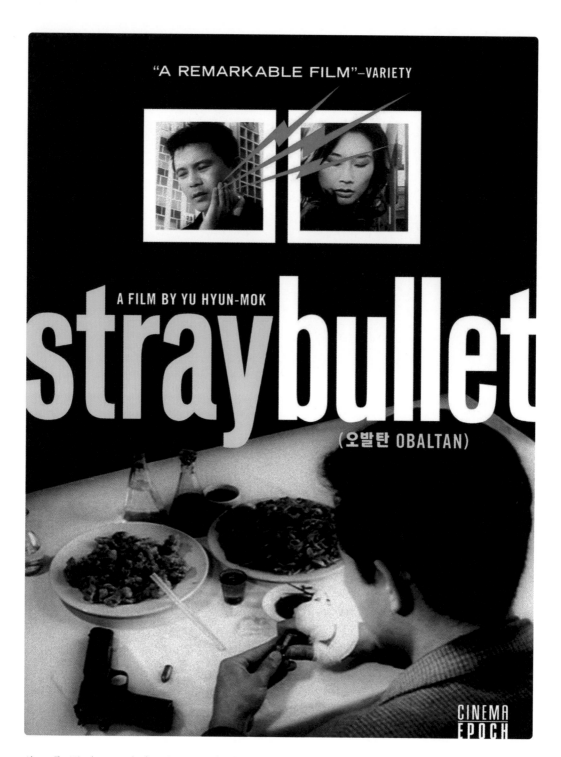

"A REMARKABLE FILM"–VARIETY

A FILM BY YU HYUN-MOK

straybullet

(오발탄 OBALTAN)

CINEMA
EPOCH

Above: The US release graphic from Cinema Epoch with the alternate (and slightly less impactful) title *Stray Bullet.*

Opposite: Another of Yu Hyun-mok's striking compositions. *Aimless Bullet*'s imagery regularly reflects its character's shadowed emotions.

AIMLESS BULLET – REVIEW

There's a recurring setting of a building site in Yu Hyun-mok's *Aimless Bullet*, but other than fraught conversation and towering bottles of booze, not much gets built. An unrelentingly bleak, hugely impressive melodrama about the pressures faced by Koreans in the post-war landscape, *Aimless Bullet* depicts a world where constructing on top of the rubble is encouraged, but finding the spirit to do so, with societal and physical wounds so close, is near impossible.

Focused on Cheolho, an accountant perennially stricken by toothache, and his unemployed brother Yeongho, Yu Hyun-mok's film follows the ex-military siblings as they navigate the battlefields of their increasingly frayed professional, romantic and domestic lives. Attempting to provide for a large family, Chul-ho (Kim Jin-kyu) trudges through the film, drawn to cash like a zombie to blood and holding his painful jaw as if it's going to fall off altogether. The angry Yeong-ho (Choi Moo-ryong), however, is more dynamic and dangerous: he storms off the set of a film that planned to exploit his battle scars for a story, starts a passionate and tragic affair with a former army nurse and barrels into a last-ditch bank robbery. Both men are trapped, either in the monotony of work, or the chase for it, but for both men daily life is an escape from their home. Theirs is a small home, crammed with responsibility, shared with demanding

children, deathly silent wives, and their PTSD-suffering mother who constantly shrieks the phrase "Let's go!" – it's no surprise that before entering the front door Cheolho has to take a breath that suggests his work is the trenches, but home is like going over the top.

Yu Hyun-mok's striking composition is a constant highlight throughout the film: using fence railings, plumbing or the scaffold of a bunk bed, he divides the frame and his characters, always keeping any meaningful connection over the precipice. Subsequently, when Yeonho's lover uses the cherry of his cigarette to light hers, the frame swells with romance thanks to the distance that's come before it. Additionally, throughout the film, intense asides enrich the drama with despair: a Christian procession, a union protest, or the shocking sight of a hanged mother with her crying baby on her back, all glimpsed and layered into the mire. As well as such visuals, *Aimless Bullet* uses sound in a way that is equally accomplished. Both sweeping and focused, the sound design lays the city in a bed of sirens, planes and shrieking, like a modern war zone; during the bank robbery, steps become kick drums and gunshots cymbals, creating a heart-racing foot chase. Yu Hyun-mok's direction transforms the bleak into the mesmeric, and the result is a powerful shot of stark melodrama that's right on target.

MOTHER AND A GUEST

사랑방 손님과 어머니

THE GO-BETWEEN

A young girl lives in a house for widows with her mother, grandmother and their maid. One day, an artist friend of her deceased father comes to stay.

1961

Director: Shin Sang-ok

102 mins

Shin Sang-ok has the peculiar honour of being known in the English-speaking world less for his films than for his fans. Well, one infamous fan in particular: North Korean dictator Kim Jong-il. Whether it's on the radio programme *This American Life*, or in Jonathan Ross's Korea-specific episode of the BBC factual series *Asian Invasion*, or even in a feature-length documentary, *The Lovers and the Despot* (2016), the story has been told time and again: in 1978, Shin and his ex-wife, the noted actress Choi Eun-hee, were abducted by North Korea under orders of the cinephile Supreme Leader, in order to stimulate the communist nation's film industry. It's quite a story, but it has succeeded in obscuring Shin's standing as one of the key filmmakers of what is described as the Golden Age of Korean Cinema.

Born in 1926 in Chongjin, which is now part of North Korea, Shin was a film fan from a young age, fondly remembering seeing the landmark Korean silent film *Arirang* (1926), as well as major international productions of the day, including Charlie Chaplin's *The Gold Rush* (1925), *Modern Times* (1936) and *The Great Dictator* (1940),

and the films of Sergei Eisenstein and D. W. Griffith. As a young man, he studied at Tokyo University of the Arts, and it was while he was in Japan that his ambitions as a filmmaker developed. In 1999, he told Adrien Gombeaud of Koreanfilm.org, "When I started studying art in Japan, I realised this vacuum in our cinema and decided to come back to Korea to rebuild Korean national cinema."

Shin entered the film industry via the art department, making props, sets and even posters, before being taken under the wing of Choi In-kyu, the director of *Hurrah! For Freedom* (1946), a major release for a country newly liberated from Japanese imperial rule. With the help of his father, a wealthy doctor who specialized in Chinese medicine, Shin made his debut as director in 1952 with the melodrama *The Evil Night*, the production of which was disrupted by the outbreak of the Korean War. One

Opposite: Take a seat. One of many contemplative moments in *Mother and a Guest*.

Below: See you in court. The central courtyard plays host to much of the film's drama.

of Shin's collaborators on that film was assistant director Yu Hyun-mok, another significant filmmaker of the period who also ended up cut off from his birthplace by the division of the country.

Shin formed a creative and romantic partnership with Choi Eun-hee after working together on the semi-documentary *Korea* (1954), and by the end of the decade, Shin was one of the country's most successful and ambitious filmmakers. 1961's *Seong Chun-hyang* was a monumental hit, attracting a 420,000-strong audience on release, and Shin swept the inaugural Grand Bell Awards in 1962, taking Best Film for the historical epic *Prince Yeonsan* and Best Director for *Mother and a Guest*. His films also screened to acclaim at international festivals such as Cannes and Berlin, where *To the Last Day* (1960) won the Extraordinary Jury Prize in 1962.

Shin then pursued his dreams of founding a major Korean film company by funnelling his energies and profits into Shin Films, which at its peak worked out of the largest studio lot in the country, producing 28 films a year with a staff of 30 directors on the payroll. It was a punishing churn, but the death knell sounded when Shin ran afoul of the authorities after a scene cut by censors from *The Rose and the Wild Dog* (1976) ended up in the film's trailer, leading Shin Films to have its production licence revoked.

Perversely, it was after the director had been abducted and "re-educated" by the North Korean regime that Shin Films was revived, with an even bigger studio and a mandate to produce quality films. However, in 1986, Shin and Choi travelled to Vienna under the pretence of meeting with potential financiers, and sought asylum at the US embassy, after which they settled in America (where Shin worked on the Disney-distributed *3 Ninjas* series of kids' martial arts comedies), before finally returning to South Korea for good in 1994.

Reflecting on his global journey, from Korea to Japan, to both sides of a divided nation, to the States and back again, Shin commented to Koreanfilm.org: "Even today when I travel with my movies in festivals and when I meet foreign people who are interested in them, I sometimes think that this might just be a big misunderstanding. For example, I'm always at the same time surprised and pleased that non-Koreans appreciate *Mother and a Guest*. But then I think that there must be something universal in every movie."

Above: Looks of longing. *Mother and a Guest* balances trials of the domestic kind with those of the heart.

Opposite top: Choi Eun-hee and Shin Sang-ok together, having safely returned from their North Korean capture.

FURTHER VIEWING 👁

The winning combination of Shin Sang-ok (pictured) and Choi Eun-hee can also be found in films such as *A Flower in Hell* (1958), *To the Last Day* (1960) and *The Memorial Gate for Virtuous Women* (1962), while Shin's North Korean monster movie, *Pulgasari* (1985), is a curious footnote to a venerable career. For another representative slice of culture-clash melodrama from Korean Cinema's Golden Age, watch director Han Hyung-mo's *Madame Freedom* (1956). Looking to the future, *Mother and a Guest* offers a child's viewpoint that anticipates two family dramas from female directors in the 21st century: Kim Bora's *House of Hummingbird* (2018) and Yoon Dan-bi's *Moving On* (2019).

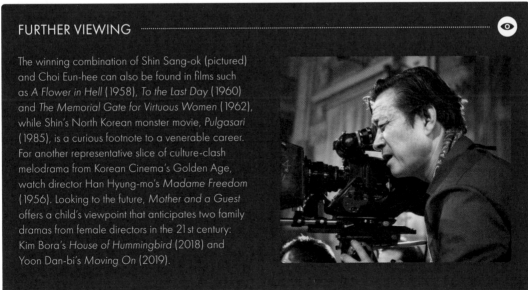

Drawn in chalk over brick and plaster, the opening credits to Shin Sang-ok's 1961 film could be graffiti tags. However, after watching this beautiful, subdued but inventive tale, you'll see that they're in fact signatures on a great work of art. *Mother and a Guest* is charming, quiet, sad and lovely, its slight story of two lonely individuals, fatefully brought together on either side of a wall, revealing not just a heartaching romance but a smart, socially engaged melodrama told in expressive, energizing style.

Coming the year after *The Housemaid*, the film offers another cautionary tale about new tenants and the potential of domestic romance. The former trades in debauchery and death, while the latter is much more reflective. Shin's film is interested less in the shock of death than in the pain of living with it, and the potential of sharing that grief. When a Christian widow (Choi Eun-hee) allows an artist, and friend of her late husband (Kim Jin-kyu), to take up residence in her home, she has to wrestle with an evolving attraction to the man, as well as the societal and religious weight of taking action on her feelings. Polite, restrained and pulsing with unspoken emotion, the two don't discuss romance, bashfully turning away from the notion. But through quiet gestures of care like the cooking of eggs, or acts of poetic expression, like passionate piano playing that lingers in their shared air, their captivation with each other speaks loudly. Mirroring the two leads are a housemaid and a local door-to-door egg salesman (also a widower, who becomes a walking reminder of fertility and family), who also become infatuated with one another. However, their vibrant personalities and proactive passion quickly develops, with the maid becoming pregnant. Their story is brisk and fervent, the former stalled by emotion.

Unsure of how society will take to a new partner, the unnamed widow finds solace in her faith, but its guidance becomes twisted by potential courtship,

her flickering excitement, fear and confusion brilliantly conveyed by Choi. She reads her Bible, but uses it to press flowers; she says the Lord's Prayer, but doesn't finish it, cutting it off when it reaches "temptation"; she wears angelic white clothes, lit dramatically against the dark wood of her home, appearing both saintly but also entirely isolated. Kim Jin-kyu, who plays the guest, shows another side of the coin to his adulterous role in *The Housemaid*, his magnetic boiling desire tempered here, and instead offering tenderness and longing, in a superb, reserved performance.

Shin's directorial approach to the story is surprisingly dynamic: instead of wading with the maudlin aspects of the story or trying to find the precisely framed everyday poetry of an Ozu drama, the film finds the playfulness and intensity of a blossoming relationship. A character getting hit by water from an emptying bucket sees the camera lens directly in the splash zone; elsewhere, as if enamoured by natural beauty the lens arcs upwards into glimmering leaves, while at moments of confusion, canted angles express the awkwardness and confusion of certain situations. Utilizing his brilliant actors, Shin makes use of close-ups to tell this story: whether via stilted dialogue, or mournful silence, these monochrome portraits pervade the film with acute yearning. Rather than viewing grief as a gap into which the shape of another person can fit, Shin's film offers a more elegant, complex outlook, with a simple resolution bravely avoided, and a more valuable, autonomous one visible through tearful eyes.

Opposite: Field day. A brief reprieve from domestic and emotional trappings.

A DAY OFF

....

휴일

BLOWING IN THE WIND

One wintry Sunday, two penniless lovers
come to the decision that they cannot
afford to start a family, leaving Huh-wook
with the task of finding money for an
abortion for the heavily pregnant Ji-youn.

1968 / 2005
Director: Lee Man-hee
73 mins

休日

製作／洪儀善

企劃／企玉淑熙 田畓

監督／李晩潔 中星一用显

脚本／由 安思淑金屋屋玉西西

—아무렇지도, 은도없고, 말랑고 보고 사랑하이있는 은 우 틈은 이기 인있 우건 거여적었인 지 거 도봐저 이 틈림이 에서 꿰있저 이들 음이 것도 가고 으고 또 오르거 그림기 있을수 없는 틈은이기 때임이……

大韓聯合映畵 株式會社作品

It's a story too perfect to resist. One of the greatest films in Korean cinema history was discovered, after being shelved for 37 years, in a dusty corner of the Korean Film Archive's warehouse. Never before screened to the public thanks to feedback from the censors that scuppered its release in 1968, *A Day Off* was finally unveiled to the world in 2005. A new classic had been found.

Born in 1931 in Seoul, Lee Man-hee was the youngest of eight children. He showed no interest in school, but loved going to the cinema – a passion that he returned to later in life after completing five years' military service, which included serving in the Korean War. He first studied acting but then landed jobs as assistant director to filmmakers such as Ahn Jong-hwa, Park Gu and Kim Myeong-je, before making his debut as a director in 1961 with *Kaleidoscope*, starring the actor Kim Seung-ho – one of the most bankable stars of the time, and the lead in the landmark drama *The Coachman* (1961), which won plaudits at the Berlin Film Festival in the same year.

Fiercely prolific in an era when directors could crank out films at an alarming rate – at his peak making 11 films in a single year – Lee enjoyed both popular success and scrutiny from censors. His 1963 Korean War drama *The Marines Who Never Returned* attracted 200,000 viewers, marking him out as a star director, yet just two years later, he ran afoul of the authorities when the initial cut of his film *The Seven Female POWs* was deemed to have violated anti-communist laws, resulting in a three-month prison sentence.

In comparison, Lee got off lightly with *A Day Off*. The powers that be deemed the film too bleak for public consumption and suggested a more positive ending: that the hopeless, lost-soul protagonist find new meaning by enlisting in the army. Lee and his backers (including producers Hong Ui-Seon and Jeon Ok-sook, parents of filmmaker Hong Sang-soo) decided it would be best to shelve the film completely.

By that point, Lee was moving towards a more experimental style, described as "cine-poems", where narrative started to take a back seat to image, technique, rhythm and mood. Unfortunately, this shift coincided with the general decline of the Korean film industry in the 1970s, and Lee soon found himself struggling for work. In 1975, he died from cirrhosis of the liver at age 45, while in post-production on what would be his last, and 51st, feature, *The Road to Sampo*. He was never fully forgotten; some of his films endured thanks to television reruns over the decades, and several appeared on the Korean Film Archive's 100 Korean Films list in 1996, but Lee's filmography proved to be ripe for rediscovery. The story of *A Day Off* is a reminder of the wonders and delights that may still be waiting for us, languishing in the archive, waiting for someone to find them.

FURTHER VIEWING 👁

The desolate, hopeless tragedy of *A Day Off* can also be found in the films of Yu Hyun-mok, including *Aimless Bullet* (1961) and *Guests Who Came by the Last Train* (1967). Lee Man-hee (pictured) made over 50 films in his short career, and was as eclectic as he was prolific, working across genres, from horror (*The Devil's Stairway*) to thrillers (*Call 112*), to noirish gangster flicks (*Black Hair*), to much less conventional, experimental films (*Assassin*). Many of his films have been restored and released by the Korean Film Archive, including two further peaks of his career, the war film *The Marines Who Never Returned* and his final work, *The Road to Sampo*.

A DAY OFF – REVIEW

Set on a Sunday, *A Day Off* opens with the imposing sight of a dark clock tower, the threat of time, its possibilities and its ending, familiar to any viewer who's stared at the slow rise of Monday's working week and dreamed of escape. Dominated by their city, its inhabitants and even the weather, Huh-Wook (Shin Seong-il) and Jee-yun's (Jeon Jee-yun) Sunday is a harsh, unrelenting urban trek into the city and the self, one compactly and ambitiously told in Lee Man-hee's controversial film.

A penniless, suited hustler roaming black-and-white streets, Huh Wook may recall Jean-Paul Belmondo's Michel in *À bout de souffle*, but unlike Michel, Huh Wook's attempted bravado feels needy, not charismatic. Despite scheming hard to get them, he gives away cigarettes to court appeal and measures the economy in café prices, an imagined flâneur whose roaming days are numbered. Unable to provide for a family, Huh Wook sets out to find money to pay for an abortion for his partner Ji-yeon. Despite struggling to converse, they are a compelling couple, the elements seemingly blowing them together. Covered in either cigarette smoke or sandstorms, they appear to have their own localized, hazy climate that thrashes and

bewilders them. Framed in stark, ultra-wide high contrast cinematography, with sparing close-ups, the couple make their way through a day that feels at times more like an Arctic expedition, their small black coats pushing through a white concrete tundra. Ji-yeon herself is even lost by the camera: in one moment after she's been left alone by Huh Wook, a considered zoom, seemingly aimed at her, crashes into the tree to her left instead, sidelining her in her own story.

Having stolen some money (in a memorable scene involving a man who, in contrast to the couple, whiles his Sunday away by taking six baths and flaunting both his hot *and* cold drinks), Huh Wook reconvenes with Ji-yeon at an abandoned factory, before they go ahead with Ji-yeon's procedure. A jagged trap of splintered wood and spiked metal, with phallic iron rods aimed at Ji-yeon from seemingly every direction, it's a dangerous, more expressionist space, compared to the barren, minimalism of the film's earlier scenes. Unforgiving to its end, the film doesn't yield from its stony philosophy, offering only cruel exits, painful memories and cold realities for sidelined, poverty-stricken women. At 73 minutes, it's a short day off, but it's one that will stay with you for a while.

Opposite top, all pictures: Gloomy Sunday. *A Day Off* depicts the bleak and hopeless existence of Korea's youth in the dark days of late-1960s Korea.

Above: Lee Man-hee incorporates the landscape and climate of the city into the action of the film, here seen dwarfing the characters and their unfortunate lives.

THE MARCH OF FOOLS

바보들의 행진

AUTUMN IS FADING, FLOWERS ARE FALLING

A group of university students lark about, look for love and dream of what the future might hold for them, all while living under the spectre of Korea's military dictatorship.

1975

Director: Ha Gil-jong

102 mins

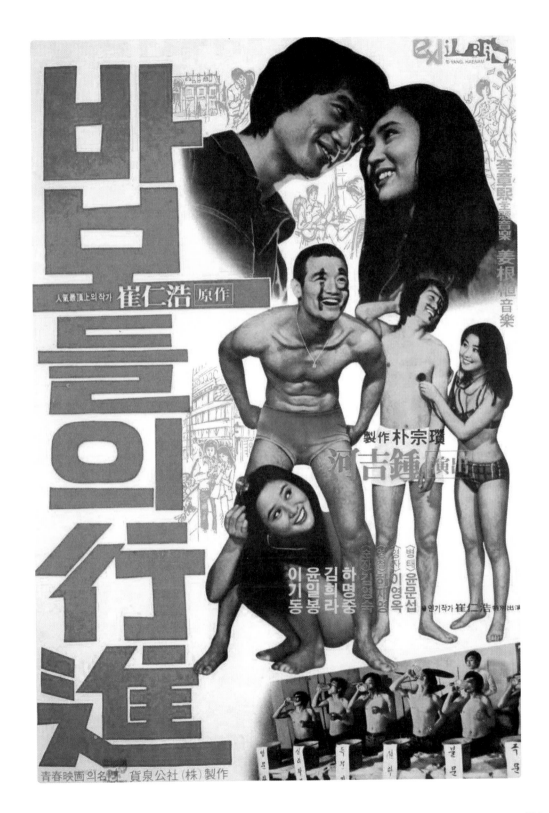

When the Korean Film Archive celebrated its 40th anniversary in 2014, it marked the occasion with a survey of 62 Korean film researchers, critics, experts and industry workers to put together a list of the Top 100 Korean films of all time. When the results were tallied, there was a three-way tie for top place: Kim Ki-young's *The Housemaid* (1960), Yu Hyun-mok's *Aimless Bullet* (1961) and Ha Gil-jong's *The March of Fools* – a bittersweet comedy set on a college campus which won acclaim and was a box office hit despite being subjected to heavy censorship on its initial release.

Tying in with the film's high placement in the Top 100 list, the Korean Film Archive released a deluxe Blu-ray set that included the censored screenplay, a number of clips that were cut from the film and the censor's report, all with the aim of helping viewers and scholars to better "understand the history of Korean film censorship". The release also stands as a tribute to director Ha Gil-jong, a fiercely radical, subversive filmmaker who had the misfortune of rising to prominence just as Korean cinema was in decline, becoming subject to its strictest period of censorship by the Park Chung-hee dictatorship, and losing considerable ground as a cultural force thanks to the popular rise of television.

Ha Gil-jong was born in Busan in 1941, the seventh child of nine. Both his parents had died by the time he was 10: his mother from illness, his father during the Korean War. He later moved to Seoul and was a promising student, studying French Literature at Seoul National University from 1959. The following years were crucial for forming his political and artistic worldview: he participated in demonstrations during 1960's April Revolution that opposed Syngman Rhee's authoritarian government; he also wrote and published poetry, and discovered a love of French cinema. But when the promise of the parliamentary Second Republic of Korea that followed the April Revolution was overthrown by a coup d'état led by Park Chung-hee in 1961, Ha and his generation found themselves on the margins. He worked for Air France, and finally moved to the United States in 1964. There, he studied at the UCLA Film School, crossed paths with New Hollywood hopefuls George Lucas and Francis Ford Coppola, and even won a nationwide student film competition that could have led to a job at MGM.

But Ha returned to Korea, with the goal of revitalizing Korean Cinema by infusing it with intellectual, auteurist, avant-garde ideas, and drawing inspiration from European arthouse cinema, the French New Wave, and

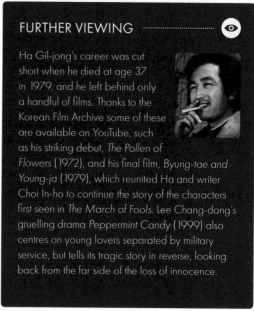

FURTHER VIEWING

Ha Gil-jong's career was cut short when he died at age 37 in 1979, and he left behind only a handful of films. Thanks to the Korean Film Archive some of these are available on YouTube, such as his striking debut, *The Pollen of Flowers* (1972), and his final film, *Byung-tae and Young-ja* (1979), which reunited Ha and writer Choi In-ho to continue the story of the characters first seen in *The March of Fools*. Lee Chang-dong's gruelling drama *Peppermint Candy* (1999) also centres on young lovers separated by military service, but tells its tragic story in reverse, looking back from the far side of the loss of innocence.

the New Hollywood, as well as directors such as Pier Paolo Pasolini and Bernardo Bertolucci. That he ultimately wasn't able to achieve his aims gives *The March of Fools*, a film itself dedicated to the thwarted potential of an ill-fated generation, an extra layer of poignance.

THE MARCH OF FOOLS – REVIEW

Anarchic, booze-soaked and occasionally very smart, *The March of Fools* is a uniquely chaotic bottling of student life. At university during Korea's military dictatorship, Byung-tae (Yoon Mun-seop) and Young-chul (Ha Jae-young) are philosophy students who chase girls instead of grades and rate beer above books, drinking in as much youthful abandon as possible to stave off inevitable military service and uncertain professional lives.

After securing tickets for blind dates with Young-ja and Sun-ja, two members of the French class, the bumbling boys scrub up and head to town, but even getting to their date is a battle: for the strict dictatorial police they encounter, their freshly styled long hair is a crime. In a chase that is just one of many slapstick misadventures, the two barrel down streets and hang from bridges, the gymnastic camerawork from cinematographer Jung Il-sung keeping up with Byung-tae and Young-chul and matching their every sprint, flip – and later, even handstand.

Having finally arrived at a dingy bar that's playing a warped version of ABBA's "Honey, Honey" (one of many great and surprising cues on the eclectic soundtrack, which brings together ballads, disco and alien synths), the pair find that their dates don't go as planned, and begin a journey into existentialism and disillusionment. Combining the frat-house bewilderment of the *National Lampoon* films, with the colour-soaked mise-en-scène and melancholic romance of *The Umbrellas of Cherbourg*, this student life is a heady cocktail of experiences. There are brash displays of insecure masculinity at drinking challenges and sports games, followed by sober reflections on their role in society, and then grand imagined plans for the future like marriage, or in the case of Young-chul, whale hunting.

As well as the disorienting look of the film, which brings inebriation to unsettling life with its wobbling zooms and shifting shallow focus, the film's sound adds to the uncanny fog of university life. ADR (automated dialogue replacement) pinpoints conversations in rowdy crowded settings, the audio's disconnection to the image giving scenes a dreamlike contrast of focus and blur, like the phrases etched in a half-constructed memory. Entering its final act, the film's unruly tone subdues, and reality bites. Inching towards the end of their time, with responsibility looming, Byung-tae and Young-chul start running, Forrest Gump style, as far as they can away from the university and their adult life, but there's no escape – the hair clippers wait for no man. From high-energy haywire beginnings, it reaches a fittingly philosophical end, which makes for a surprisingly moving watch. Like many students looking back on their time at university, viewers will look in fondness and horror at the mayhem of *The March of Fools*, and they might get a lesson as well.

Opposite top: From ruthless inductions, to existential endings, *The March of Fools* deeply probes university life.

Below left and right: Balancing a romantic storyline and the farce of performed masculinity, Ha Gil-jong's film is as moving as it is provoking.

SUDDENLY IN THE DARK

깊은밤 갑자기

A DOLL'S HOUSE

A woman starts to believe her husband is having an affair with their young housekeeper, who has brought a strange wooden doll into their home.

1981

Director: Go Yeong-nam

95 mins

Above: Ready maid. With its creepy, controlling housekeeper character, *Suddenly in the Dark* riffs on Kim Ki-young's 1960 thriller, *The Housemaid*.

Below: Knife or death. Arriving in the wake of John Carpenter's *Halloween*, *Suddenly in the Dark* exhibits some potential influence from the rise of slasher-horror.

While Korean cinema declined as a popular art form across the 1970s, due to varying factors including the rise of television and continued interference from strict government censors, many films continued to be made every year. Directors and production companies still churned out product, often with insufficient budget (or time) for such things as quality or artistic ambition. Some, such as director Im Kwon-taek, eventually found their creative voice within the scrum, but others were beholden to the grind.

Director Go Yeong-nam was one such director. Born in 1935, Go is one of the most (if not the most) prolific filmmakers in Korean cinema history, directing 110 films in genres ranging from action movies to melodramas from his debut in 1964 until his death in 2003. In the words of his frequent collaborator, the producer David Suh, Go was something of a workhorse: competent, flexible, versatile and free of ego. He was one of the best filmmakers in the country at time when simply getting the job done was one of the most prized attributes a director could have.

Suddenly in the Dark, also known as *Suddenly at Midnight* or *Suddenly in Dark Night*, was Go's sole horror film, and benefitted from a gentle easing of censorship in the early 1980s with regard to nudity and violence, which allowed the film to ride in the slipstream of popular American slasher flicks such as John Carpenter's *Halloween* (1978). Essentially a riff on Kim Ki-young's *The Housemaid* (1960), yet with more explicit flourishes, Hitchcockian voyeurism, and a heady dose of kaleidoscopic, shamanic horror added in for good measure, *Suddenly in the Dark* came and went in 1981. It was released on VHS and even played on Korean television in edited form, but was mostly forgotten, until the Korean Film Archive restored the film over three decades later. Screenings at the Bucheon International Fantastic Film Festival, KOFA's own Cinematheque and the Asian Film Archive in Singapore followed, as did a Blu-ray release from the American cult cinema label Mondo Macabro, which heralded the film as a rediscovered classic of Korean horror, the missing link between Kim Ki-young and the rise of K-horror in the late 1990s.

A diamond had been found in the rough, challenging some presumptions about the history of Korean horror cinema. Film critic Darcy Paquet, on the occasion of the film's screening at Udine's Far East Film Festival in 2021, wrote: "Korean horror films from the 70s and 80s can be memorable, fascinating, and at times even cute, but they are rarely frightening. *Suddenly in the Dark* is an exception."

Top right: Deep blue. The vivid colours of *Suddenly in the Dark* evoke the bold stylisation of Italian horror legend, Dario Argento.

FURTHER VIEWING 👁

The genuinely creepy closing sequence of *Suddenly in the Dark* (directed by Go Yeong-nam, pictured) points to later K-horror hits like *Whispering Corridors* (1998), *A Tale of Two Sisters* (2003) and *The Wailing* (2016), which crop up later in this book. *Suddenly in the Dark* also leads us away from Korea to the lurid delights of Italian maestro Dario Argento's colourful, supernatural horror films *Suspiria* (1977) and *Inferno* (1980). Despite the gloomy depiction of mainstream Korean cinema described above, many filmmakers did make their mark in the 1980s, including Im Kwon-taek with his breakthrough Buddhist monk drama *Mandala* (1981), Lee Jang-ho with *A Fine, Windy Day* (1980) and *Declaration of Idiot* (1983), Bae Chang-ho with a series of commercial hits including the beloved road movie *Whale Hunting* (1984), and the directors who would form what is described as the Korean New Wave, including Park Kwang-su (*Chilsu and Mansu*, 1988) and Jang Sun-woo (*The Age of Success*, 1988).

SUDDENLY IN THE DARK – REVIEW

Chucky, Annabelle, M3gan. They're child's play to this dollhouse of horrors. *Suddenly in the Dark*, a lurid, romping relative to Korean classic *The Housemaid*, is about Seon-hee (Kim Young-ae), a professor's wife, and her distrust of new, young home help Mi-ok (Lee Ki-seon), and the potentially possessed, knife-wielding wooden idol she carries with her.

Seon-hee's husband Kang Yu-jin (Yoon Il-bong) studies butterflies, his pristinely framed specimens lining the walls of their isolated country house, a vision of both rural domestic bliss and feminine entrapment. (Peter Strickland's other-worldly erotic drama *The Duke of Burgundy* (2014) similarly plays out a psychosexual tête-à-tête in a rural home adorned with butterflies.)

Decorated in extremely saturated colours, the home that Yu-jin invites Mi-ok into is an uncanny creation, the perfect, brightly lit set at artificial odds to the exterior greenery. Featuring red carpets, chairs, flowers and even golf bags, it's an enjoyably unsubtle staging ground for a war of passion to turn bloody. Seon-hee initially welcomes Mi-ok, but after seeing her naked youth (the camera hurling on to its side to gawp at the full length of her legs) she starts to unravel, her concerns over ageing and body image embodied in her new houseguest. Mi-ok is having an

illicit affair with her husband, she imagines (or maybe she doesn't), under the puppeteering of the doll, and things eventually turn violent and deadly.

Regularly shot through kaleidoscopic lens filters, *Suddenly in the Dark* offers a lot of fun thanks to its playful form, regularly refracting and duplicating Seon-hee's terror with disorienting practical effects – and even a quick nod to *The Shining*'s door-axing moment. One recurring visual, shot between the arcing taxidermied heads of two snakes, frames characters in the shape of a love heart, the fangs of suspicion primed to poison. Beyond the look of the film, the extreme sound treatment, like reverb effects on dialogue, adds to Seon-hee's distancing from reality, while the score, which clashes synth throbs with classical melodies, has the wonderfully unnerving feeling of Tchaikovsky via Goblin.

Seon-hee will never be one of her husband's butterflies, trapped and pinned against a wall, frozen at their most beautiful. Go's film, which is cine-literate but never smug, has its schlocky thrills, but underpinning them all is an engrossing, and quite sad, story about feminine expectation, isolation and jealousy. A dazzling prismatic dream full of carnal nightmares, *Suddenly in the Dark* is riotous, righteous viewing.

Opposite: Fatal attraction. Due to a relaxation in Korean cinema censorship, *Suddenly in the Dark* was allowed to indulge in more overt erotic scenes.

Above: Dolly mixture. The kaleidoscopic optical effects deployed during *Suddenly in the Dark*'s wildest scenes are a dizzying highlight.

SEOPYEONJE

서편제

FOLK TALE

Following the liberation of Korea from Japanese imperial rule at the end of the Second World War, a family of musicians that perform traditional *pansori* folk songs struggle to maintain a living for themselves amid the modernization and Westernization of the country.

1993

Director: Im Kwon-taek

112 mins

임권택 감독작품

서편제

SOPYONJE

On 10 April 1993, *Seopyeonje* opened in a single-screen cinema in Seoul. By the end of the year, it had sold one million tickets, landing just shy of the biggest Hollywood imports of the year: *Jurassic Park* and *Cliffhanger*. It was the largest turnout for a Korean film in history, setting a benchmark that would last for most of the rest of the decade, until *Shiri* ushered in a new era of homemade blockbusters in 1999. The release was a watershed moment, but the director behind this surprise hit wasn't a young gun, he was an old hand.

Born in 1934, Im Kwon-taek entered the film industry in Seoul as an apprentice in 1955, working his way up from dogsbody to director via the production and props departments, eventually assisting director Jeong Chang-hwa. Im learned the fundamentals of filmmaking from Jeong, a successful genre filmmaker who would go on to work in Hong Kong, directing *King Boxer* (1972, also known as *Five Fingers of Death*) for the legendary Shaw Brothers studio.

Im himself made his debut in 1962 at the age of 28 with the war film *Farewell to the Duman River*, which proved to be a hit. However, unlike older, more ambitious filmmakers such as Shin Sang-ok, Yu Hyun-mok and Lee Man-hee – three directors he once modestly said he couldn't possibly hold a candle to – Im was swallowed up by the mainstream filmmaking machine, cranking out features to order as a hired hand. Within his first decade as a filmmaker, Im made 45 films, in various genres, ranging from melodramas to martial arts flicks, comedies to Manchurian Westerns (a Korean spin on that most American of genres). Basically, he made whatever the production company required. "In those days, I made a movie just like going into an office to work every day," he recalled in the book *Im Kwon-taek Speaks of Im Kwon-taek*. "I just made films to earn a living. I wasn't even conscious of being a director then."

Looking back in May 2002 in conversation with French film critic Michel Ciment, he described his early films as "lemons". He went even further when speaking with *Time Out Singapore* in 2014, saying they were simply bad movies. "I was immature when I first started," he explained. "But I started becoming more mature and regretting those bad films I made; I thought my films should be changed,

Above: Oh Jung-hae as Song-hwa, the lead singer in the film's *pansori* duo.

Opposite top: Drum roll. A traditional *gosu* performance provides an early education.

FURTHER VIEWING

Following *Seopyeonje*'s surprise box office success, Im Kwon-taek (pictured) would return to similar territory over the years, with smaller returns but growing international renown. 2000's *Chunhyang* is a direct adaptation of a *pansori* work, and was the first Korean film to screen in competition at the Cannes film festival; 2002's *Chi-hwa-seon*, which focused on Korean painting, also screened at Cannes and netted Im the Best Director prize. Conversely, 2007's *Beyond the Years*, Im's 100th feature, which was touted as a pseudo-sequel to *Seopyeonje*, failed to bring in the punters. For another film from the period that uses cinema to explore Korean culture, look to Bae Yong-kyun's *Why Has Bodhi-Dharma Left for the East?* (1989), a meditation on Korean Seon Buddhism that was a minor hit at home, but travelled widely, screening at Cannes and picking up the Golden Leopard at the Locarno International Film Festival.

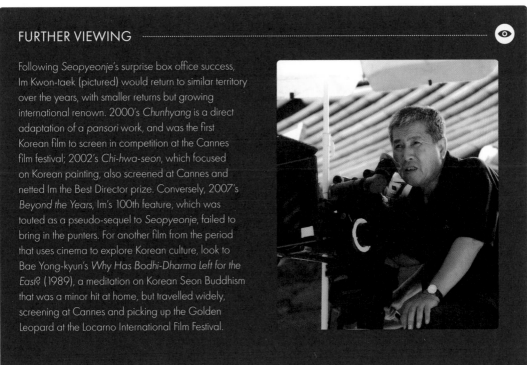

which then led me to make films that expressed and demonstrated the real life and emotions of Koreans."

A major milestone came in 1981 with the Buddhist monk drama *Mandala*, which was simultaneously an artistic breakthrough, a hit at home, and a festival favourite abroad after a screening at the Berlin Film Festival in 1982. During the ensuing decade, Im became one of the most visible and well-regarded Korean filmmakers on the world stage. *Gilsoddeum* (1986) also screened in Berlin, and *The Surrogate Woman* (1987) competed at the Venice Film Festival, with star Kang Soo-yeon winning the Best Actress Prize.

But then came *Seopyeonje*. Initially planned as something of an indulgent passion project after the much more commercial gangster action of the *General's Son* trilogy (1990–1992), the film proved to be an unprecedented success. An artfully composed drama about the declining fortunes of a family of Korean *pansori* folk-song performers, it caught the zeitgeist at a time where Korean cultural identity was a hot topic. It also set in motion many of the transmedia tie-ins that we now expect from a blockbuster, birthing the first original soundtrack release and first book dedicated to a single Korean film.

After his decade of making dozens of lemons, and a lifetime finding his filmmaking voice, Im Kwon-taek had a clear mission. In *The Cinema of Japan and Korea*, Im told the academic Han Ju Kwak: "My personal desire has been to capture elements of our traditional culture in my work. The fear is that those aspects of Korean culture may be absorbed and, in the end, disappear."

Above: Look out. As *Seopyeonje* evolves, the biological relationship between sound and vision gets exploited.

Below: "If You Want to Sing Out, Sing Out." A rare moment of musical harmony for *Seopyeonje*'s central family.

Opposite: Shot in a variety of natural landscapes, the film's cinematography is one of *Seopyeonje*'s many striking aspects.

SEOPYEONJE – REVIEW

Quietly nursing wounds, plotting revenge, recounting heroic moments – these are the kinds of reactions film characters might typically have to being on the other end of a beating. In *Seopyeonje*, the obsessive musician and teacher Yu-bong (Kim Myung-gon) finds inspiration, revering the vocal quality of the man who just socked him. It's a surprising, darkly comic beat, but one that illustrates his addiction to his craft, and his willingness to suffer for it. To him, penance pays the entry to higher musical planes, a philosophy that does lead to undeniably beautiful songs, but at a cost that shatters his family.

Told predominantly in flashback, the film is framed by the journey of Dong-ho (Kim Kyu-chul), a smartly dressed man from the city, who has ventured out to the countryside in an attempt to reconnect with his sister Song-hwa (Oh Jung-hae). Slipping back from the 1960s to Dong-ho's youth, the film's bulk tells the story of a non-biological family, formed of widows and orphans, Dong-ho, Song-hwa and their dictatorial adoptive father Yu-bong, who sees his newly acquired children as a passage to musical ascension. Chasing neither fortune or fame, Yu-bong wants to fight back against the *Westernization* of popular music, and repopularize *pansori* – a traditional Korean style of singing, featuring a solo vocalist and drummer, or *gosu*. Travelling for work, across cold wide fields and thick burnt-orange woodland (the striking, but never overly staged, cinematography is by Jung Il-sung, who also worked on *The March of Fools*), Yu-bong terrorizes his protégés with endless singing and drumming lessons; at times the film feels like a Terence Malick version of *Whiplash*. Their songs tell transportive, melancholic fables, the simplicity of the set-up highlighting the skill in Song-hwa's haunting, undulating tones and Dong-ho's punctuating taps. Harassed by their father, they arrive in towns in dusty hanbok clothing, looking more like refugees than performers, and are treated like jesters, out of time with the brass bands, suits and ties of post-war Korea.

There are moments of uninhibited pleasure for the group: during a superb extended take, their wandering voices emerge from a field prior to their arrival in shot, as if the song is coming from the ground itself. It's a rare portion of joy, with the family improvising their own lyrics and injecting themselves into a song, briefly, personally, becoming part of the musical history Yu-bong longs for them to be in. But it's not enough. Yu-bong's abuse increases, the family splinters, and a shocking, selfish act is enacted with fearsome and irreconcilable ease.

Throughout the film, characters encounter a calligrapher, who draws people's names in rich colours, adorning the letters with illustrations of vibrant wildlife. His is an entirely different art form to music, and the calligrapher's hand has no victim: in painting for Song-hwa, he gives her name beauty, written on paper that she hugs close. It's a moment that hands her some agency, and by the end of the film the siblings are able to take ownership of their combined musical skill, and powerfully discard it. Never shying away from the untreatable fractures of their abuse and its tangle with their talent, the film's final notes offer reassurance, even without the prospect of harmony.

BAD MOVIE

나쁜 영화

LIVING ON THE EDGE

Using an experimental and often uncompromising blend of fiction and documentary, director Jang Sun-woo compiles a series of episodes inspired by the lives of Seoul's homeless, hopeless and delinquent young people.

1997

Director: Jang Sun-woo

125 mins

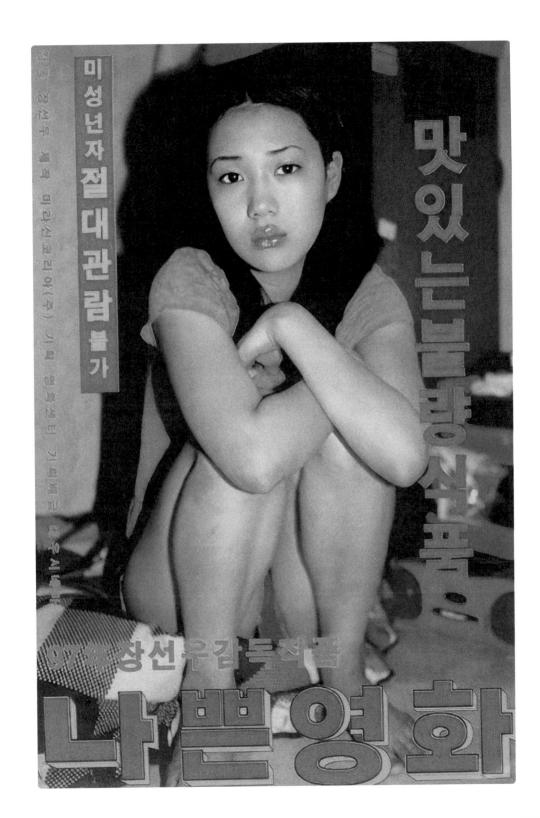

Born in 1952, Jang Sun-woo (pictured bottom right) is a member of the generation that was irrevocably marked by the turbulent political climate of their youth. While he was a student in Seoul National University, he participated in and organized demonstrations against Korea's military government, resulting in him being arrested and spending six months in prison. Afterwards, Jang was inspired to turn to filmmaking when he saw Lee Jang-ho's *A Fine, Windy Day* (1980), and when he started making his own features, they were unpredictable, transgressive and confrontational, from the corporate satire *The Age of Success* (1988) to *A Petal* (1996), a disturbing meditation on the lingering national trauma following the Gwangju Uprising of 1980.

Bad Movie – or *Timeless, Bottomless Bad Movie* to give it its full, international title – is pretty much what it says on the tin. A self-consciously experimental, explicit and violent film that is often extremely hard to watch. Shot on the streets of Seoul, the film features several episodes starring real kids, playing themselves, with footage shot on 16mm and 35mm film as well as digital video, providing a sensory overload of film styles.

Film critic Tony Rayns, reporting on the film's release for *Sight and Sound* in 1998, called it "the most provocative Korean film yet", before describing a moral panic that gripped the country in 1997, following a scandal where it had been discovered that certain high schoolers had been making their own porn films. In response there was greater scrutiny across the arts. Authors were jailed, and the queer romantic drama *Happy Together*, directed by Hong Kong auteur Wong Kar-wai, was refused a distribution licence. Jang Sun-woo and *Bad Movie*, in comparison, had an easier ride: the film was released in cinemas with 20 minutes cut by the Korean Ethics Committee, while an uncut version screened at festivals in Busan and Tokyo.

Following *Bad Movie*'s controversy-stricken release, Jang would go on to make two further movies, *Lies* (1999) and *Resurrection of the Little Match Girl* (2002), which enjoyed wider international distribution. The former was a continuation of the director's interest in experimental, explicit filmmaking, but the latter was touted as a commercial, action-packed popcorn spectacle – and yet it bombed on release, and Jang has been in creative exile ever since.

However, whether you chalk it up to a morbid fascination for the weird, the gnarly and the extreme, or a borrowed nostalgia for 1990s aesthetics and esoterica, *Bad Movie* has endured thanks to film fan communities that like to sail through the murky waters of file sharing, torrenting and other shady means to embrace all that

FURTHER VIEWING

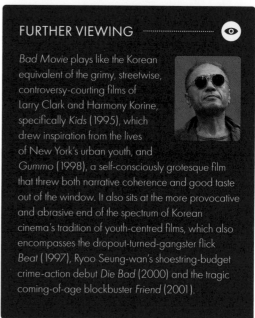

Bad Movie plays like the Korean equivalent of the grimy, streetwise, controversy-courting films of Larry Clark and Harmony Korine, specifically *Kids* (1995), which drew inspiration from the lives of New York's urban youth, and *Gummo* (1998), a self-consciously grotesque film that threw both narrative coherence and good taste out of the window. It also sits at the more provocative and abrasive end of the spectrum of Korean cinema's tradition of youth-centred films, which also encompasses the dropout-turned-gangster flick *Beat* (1997), Ryoo Seung-wan's shoestring-budget crime-action debut *Die Bad* (2000) and the tragic coming-of-age blockbuster *Friend* (2001).

world cinema has to offer. On the film-logging community Letterboxd, a bastion of online cinephilia that is gently subverting the canon, *Bad Movie* has found a new audience, cropping up often in creatively named lists of films lovingly crafted by its users, with evocative titles such as "I'm just a kid and life is a nightmare", "how to get mad letterboxd cred" and "cinema for the deeply disturbed".

BAD MOVIE – REVIEW

The title page for this chapter says that Jang Sun-Woo is the filmmaker behind *Timeless, Bottomless Bad Movie*, but the film itself is less clear, its screeching opening collage simply saying "Not fixed" next to various credits. Telling the story of – or perhaps being told by – a collection of violent youths in central Seoul, this fascinating, chaotic film is a kaleidoscope of destruction, abuse and empathy.

It features freewheeling, neon-coloured, terror-reigning teenagers, and fans of Harmony Korine's work will feel comfortably uncomfortable in this carnage of creativity and excess. Smashing together episodes from the different members of a friendship group, ranging from an anarchic trip to a bowling alley, to a session of fume-huffing and oral sex, the snapshot scrapbook narrative is almost as frenetic as the film's form. Keeping reality at a blur, a camera crew will pop up in some scenes, asking the friends questions or, in one moment that recalls the wailing teen motorbike gangs of *Akira*, even getting run over. Alongside the gang's stories are recurring interviews with homeless people living in Seoul Station. These slower, more contemplative moments don't just give the film necessary breaths, but the clarity and complexity of the discussions, especially around addiction, family and sex are also incredibly moving.

Mixing over-the-shoulder documentary style, with shot-from-the-hip voyeurism, there's a gritty realism to *Bad Movie*, something that thrillingly splinters against the stylization of the rest of the film. Mixing phallic stop-motion moments, punk title cards with text like "Korean National Anthem" or "Plagiarism", infographic quizzes about runaway young people and even a section designed like a side scrolling video game, *Bad Movie* is a relentless, graphic (in more ways than one) viewing experience. Recalling the legendary editor/sound designer Walter Murch, whose "worldizing" shaped the sonically overloaded youth culture of *American Graffiti*, the sound of *Bad Movie* is feverishly impressive too, with pop music, traffic sounds and arcade bleeps all stirring up the atmosphere. Huge credit must also go to editor Kim Yong-soo, whose assembly mixes, repeats and refreshes its own shape throughout, while also managing to maintain constant narrative propulsion.

Its overture says the film is "All done spontaneously. It's nothing serious", but scenes of drug, alcohol and physical abuse mean that there are controversial moments throughout the film – none more so than an act of group sexual assault at the film's end. Exhausting, awful and long, the scene is then immediately followed by the actors discussing its staging. Confounding to its end, constantly pulling back curtains and holding up mirrors, this film, whoever made it, really is timeless.

Opposite top: Mirror image. To make *Bad Movie*, director Jang Sun-woo put the camera into the hands of kids themselves.

Above left and right: Bright young things. *Bad Movie* races through the colour spectrum and holds up a mirror to confused and angry members of Seoul's youth.

CHRISTMAS IN AUGUST

8월의 크리스마스

A DEVELOPING ROMANCE

Thirty-something photo shop owner Jung-won starts a tentative friendship with young parking officer Da-rim, which could blossom into something more – but then he receives a troubling, terminal diagnosis.

1998

Director: Hur Jin-ho

97 mins

8월의
크리스마스

사랑을 간직한 채 떠나갔던
그 사람이 다시 돌아옵니다

한석규 심은하

2013.11.6

When charting the birth of a new generation of Korean filmmakers and cinemagoers in the late 1990s and early 2000s, industry expert Darcy Paquet notes a rise in both cinephilia and cineliteracy. The state-supported Korean Academy of Film Arts trained a new crop of talented young filmmakers, including Bong Joon-ho, Im Sang-soo and Jang Joon-hwan, and inspired other higher education institutions to implement similar courses geared towards film production. Meanwhile, a new generation was engaging with cinema with passion and curiosity. European cinema and arthouse filmmakers were popular with this young crowd, from Leos Carax and Wong Kar-Wai to Andrei Tarkovsky and Abbas Kiarostami. There was a boom in video rental stores, film festivals and film magazines like *Kino* and *Cine21* (the latter eventually becoming Korea's bestselling weekly magazine). The stage was set for a wave of new Korean cinema.

Director Hur Jin-ho was born in 1963 in Jeonju, and studied philosophy at Yonsei University in Seoul before enrolling in the Korean Academy of Film Arts. While he loved watching films as a kid, and even worked as a film critic for a time, he didn't consider himself a hardened cinephile. After graduating, he worked with Korean New Wave pioneer Park Kwang-su as assistant director on two key films of the decade: 1993's *To the Starry Island* and 1995's *A Single Spark* (both co-written by Lee Chang-dong).

It was after wrapping the latter film, while on holiday in France, that Hur discovered the filmmaker who would become one of his biggest inspirations when embarking on his first forays into features. As he recalled in 2006 to Asiexpo, he happened to be in Paris while there was a retrospective of the work of Japanese director Yasujirō Ozu – a filmmaker he hadn't encountered before: "It was a real discovery for me... I was largely influenced by these seemingly innocuous little stories of people like you and

Opposite: Hur Jin-ho's focused portrait of a photographer was a box office success and a star maker.

Above: The photo shop around the corner. Jung-won's place of work is the film's warm and welcoming primary location.

Below: One of many shared food moments. In *Christmas in August* characters regularly unite over a meal.

me, whose ordinary daily life can still lead us to reflect on the depth of life and make a very great film." Not long after watching Ozu's films, Hur began work on what would become his feature debut, *Christmas in August*, inspired in part by the Japanese filmmaker's simplicity of storytelling and stripped-back filmmaking style.

On release in 1998, *Christmas in August* was a runaway success. In Seoul alone, it sold over 400,000 tickets, and ended the year as one of most popular Korean films at the domestic box office, and later had success both in Hong Kong and Japan (where it was remade in 2005). It was a prizewinner, too, taking home Best Film, Best New Director (shared with Im Sang-soo), Best Cinematography and Best Actress at the Blue Dragon Film Awards, and Best New Director, Best Screenplay and a Special Jury Prize from the Grand Bell Awards. The film also travelled to the Cannes Film Festival, screening in the Critics' Week parallel selection alongside debut works from rising filmmakers such as François Ozon, Gaspar Noé and Andrea Arnold.

Darcy Parquet chalks up the popular success of *Christmas in August* to the evergreen appeal of the melodrama, a staple of Korean film, but draws attention to the ways that Hur and his contemporaries achieved a sort of "aesthetic renewal" by taking time-honoured genres and reinventing them for a new era and audience, finding "meaning and beauty in spaces that Korean cinema had previously overlooked".

FURTHER VIEWING 👁

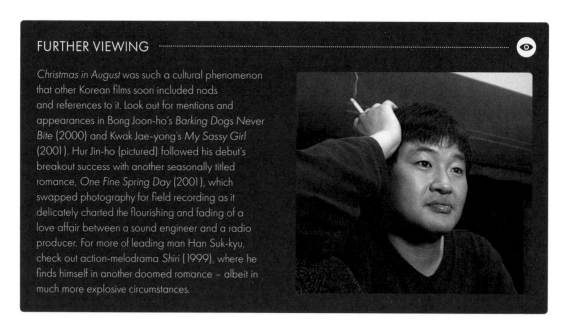

Christmas in August was such a cultural phenomenon that other Korean films soon included nods and references to it. Look out for mentions and appearances in Bong Joon-ho's *Barking Dogs Never Bite* (2000) and Kwak Jae-yong's *My Sassy Girl* (2001). Hur Jin-ho (pictured) followed his debut's breakout success with another seasonally titled romance, *One Fine Spring Day* (2001), which swapped photography for field recording as it delicately charted the flourishing and fading of a love affair between a sound engineer and a radio producer. For more of leading man Han Suk-kyu, check out action-melodrama *Shiri* (1999), where he finds himself in another doomed romance – albeit in much more explosive circumstances.

CHRISTMAS IN AUGUST – REVIEW

One of the most gentle and most affecting films in this book, *Christmas in August* is perhaps the furthest it is possible to get from the reductive, "extreme" perception of Korean cinema held in the West in the late 1990s. Hur Jin-ho's film, and its central setting, move at their own slight, warm pace. Full of patient, rewarding image-making, *Christmas in August* unfurls with the same revelatory joy and melancholy inherent in poring over a long-awaited, freshly developed pack of photos.

Following a terminally ill photographer and shop owner Jung-won, his blossoming romance with parking officer Da-rim and its subsequent dismantling, *Christmas in August* is a wonder of a film that offers reassurance in the face of mortality, hope in heartbreak and knowledge that an ice lolly on a hot day is an unparalleled gift. Director Hur Jin-ho captures the precise but exploratory nature of a photographer's life: we see Jung-won carefully pose his clients in his studio, and observe the unpredictable flow of life around him, through the lenses of his shop, bus and hospital windows, exerting control where he can but embracing what he can't. Much like Japanese director Hirokazu Kore-eda's masterpiece *After Life*, set in a limbo where memories must be recreated as film scenes, *Christmas in August* uses the experiences of being in front of and behind the lens as a way to navigate and accept death, via the joys of life.

The heart of the film is the stoic, almost irrepressibly smiley Han Suk-kyu, whose performance as Jung-won could be gratingly optimistic, but instead gl≠≠≠ows with a softer, affirmative positivity that enchants the film, provoking its greatest joys and sorrows. Opposite Han is Shim Eun-ha as Da-rim, whose journey from intrigue, to adoration, to devastation stays endearing and grounded, eschewing the narrative's melodramatic sensibility. The chemistry between the two is natural and gleefully silly, from their clumsy sharing of an icy treat to a swoon-worthy conversation navigated around the topic of suicide and farts.

Hur's prowess as a visual storyteller is, fittingly in this tale about a photographer, on show here. Imbuing the

Opposite top: Framed through his camera or around windows, Jung-won has a photographer's observational outlook on the world.

Above: Breezy rider. Although built around a tragic event, *Christmas in August* maintains a bright outlook.

film's rhythm with Jung-won's patient eye, the camera unwaveringly lingers on faces, in particular their smiles, holding a little long like the posed grins of a school photo. The bright, saturated lighting of a perfectly lit portrait seeps into the outside world too, making the mundane gleam, as if Jung-won is discovering that perfect imagery is available to him at all times, not just for his photographs. Long, unbroken and absorbing takes let life unfold in front of the image, whether that's a wide shot chronicling shopfront activity, or the giddy eating of a watermelon and spitting of its seeds. Hur's image-led storytelling is most rewarding in the final act of the film, which plays as a remarkable, almost dialogue-free symphony, with upset, healing, demise and acceptance all translated through looks, touches and, of course, a smile for the camera. Although built around a shop and a romance that wouldn't exist in a digital age, *Christmas in August* is timeless, its wisdom rich and welcoming, its artistic expertise unfaded.

WHISPERING CORRIDORS

여고괴담

SCHOOL OF SHOCK

When rumours circulate that the ghost of a pupil is terrorizing the staff and students of a high school, one of the deceased girl's former friends, now a teacher herself, starts to investigate.

1998

Director: Park Ki-hyung

105 mins

For British film fans of a certain age, Korean cinema will have a near unshakable association with the phrase "Asia Extreme". The term was popularized in the early 2000s by the theatrical and home video distributor Tartan Films, which gathered together films from across the continent to create a manufactured cultural moment. This loosely defined but wildly successful brand encompassed everything from explosive thrillers to gory slashers to unclassifiable oddities, including films as diverse and disparate as *The Ring*, *Audition*, *Battle Royale* and *Dark Water* from Japan, *The Eye* and *Infernal Affairs* from Hong Kong and, from Korea, the likes of *Shiri*, *Save the Green Planet!*, *A Tale of Two Sisters* and *Oldboy*.

It's therefore ironic, perhaps, that in the years preceding Tartan Films' touting of Asia as the home of cutting-edge cult cinema, the horror genre in particular was out of fashion in Korea, despite a tradition dating back decades to the work of Kim Ki-young and beyond. Horror's resurgence in the country as both a creative canvas and a money-spinner has been in part credited to the success of 1998's *Whispering Corridors*, a deeper cut in the Asia Extreme library.

Producer Oh Ki-min initially had a hard time finding backers for his proposal for a ghost story set in a high school, which drew inspiration from British filmmaker Lindsay Anderson's anti-establishment boarding-school satire *If...* (1968). Eventually, he found a willing collaborator in producer Lee Choon-yun of the production company Cine2000, who recalled the box office success of the 1995 Japanese horror *Gakkō no kaidan* (aka *School Ghost Stories*, or *Haunted School*), and thought a similar film could do well in Korea. What sweetened the deal was that it could be made quickly and cost-effectively: *Whispering Corridors* was assigned a two-month shooting schedule, and a production budget of under $600,000.

The producers agreed that the project was the perfect testing ground for a hungry newcomer, and the director's job was given to Park Ki-hyung, who was fresh off finishing an award-winning horror short, *Great Pretenders*. Born in 1967, Park wasn't much of a film fan as a kid, growing up in the era when the Korean movie industry was in popular decline. He studied engineering at college, and became interested in filmmaking only via his passions for music and photography. In fact, he confessed to the Korean Film Council that he didn't seriously watch films until he was in his early twenties, saying: "I often thought films were just a form of low-class popular culture." A viewing of Gillo Pontecorvo's influential war film *The Battle of Algiers* (1966) changed everything. Later, he became infatuated with American cinema – films such as *Vertigo*, *Easy Rider*,

FURTHER VIEWING

Following the success of the 1998 film, producer Lee Choon-yun developed *Whispering Corridors* into an umbrella franchise that explored similar supernatural horror themes in all-girl high-school environments, united by the credo "different directors, different stories, different settings, different schools" – including fan favourites *Memento Mori* (1999) and *Wishing Stairs* (2003). He steered the series until he passed away in May 2021, the month before the release of the sixth *Whispering Corridors* film, *The Humming*. Since the turn of the millennium, horror has been a fertile genre for Korean cinema, with highlights ranging from *A Tale of Two Sisters* (also produced by Oh Ki-min) to *The Wailing*, which are both discussed later in this book. For a twisted depiction of the male experience of the Korean education system, track down Yeon Sang-ho's violent, grotesque animated feature, *The King of Pigs*.

and especially *Blue Velvet* – describing himself as a devoted David Lynch fan.

Making *Whispering Corridors* may have been a risk, but the fates were in its favour. In the late 1990s, all signs pointed to a rebirth of Korean national cinema as a popular art form. Academic Jinhee Choi writes that a key factor was the opening of Korea's first chain of multiplex cinemas. When *Whispering Corridors* opened in May 1998, it played at eight of the eleven screens at the brand-new CGV multiplex in Seoul. On release, it scared more than 2 million cinemagoers and ended the year one of the highest-grossing Korean films at the domestic box office.

WHISPERING CORRIDORS – REVIEW

For anyone who didn't really fit in at school, the blood-soaked, squirming anxiety of *Whispering Corridors* might feel less like a horror film, and more like a smartly observed social drama. Park Ki-hyung's film reckons with the trauma factory of education, the poison of gossip and the spiritual power of self-expression, all via a deliciously over-the-top ghost story.

When a notoriously cruel teacher, nicknamed Old Fox, is found dead in a gruesome and mysterious fashion, the students of Jookran High School for Girls must endure the looming threat of her ghostly killer, as well as the corporal punishments of the man they call Mad Dog, the leering substitute Mr Oh. The students are unknowingly thrown into a fight for social and physical survival, against the violence of their inhumane teacher, and the spectre of a student, killed at the school a decade prior and now taking vengeance.

The horror of *Whispering Corridors*, despite the branding it was given, isn't always "extreme". Offering schlocky thrills and throbbing unease, Park injects fear in stabs and waves; there are moments of violence but the pervading nervousness that underpins every scene is what makes the film so scary. Park's love for David Lynch's brand of offset societal terror is clear: from the bright, saturated soap-opera lighting, to the regular ominous whooshing on the soundtrack, to the slim borders between purity and the demonic, Jookran could be twinned with the town of Twin Peaks. Highlighting how one horrific act can shatter and haunt a community, across many years, the *Whispering*

Corridors of the title are both a weapon and a curse. The school hallways are a home to gossip, bullying and repression, which causes dire consequences; they're also the haunt of unsettled spirits looking for retribution, luring unseemly characters to their doom. One particularly satisfying slice of gleeful gore comes when Mad Dog, having previously insisted that "a woman should be like cotton candy", is disposed of sweetly.

The mischievous cinematography, by Seo Jeong-min, keeps apace with the piling body count and the pupil's twisting mental state: distorting zooms and aerial positions give the familiar school space a sense of unreality, while a *Halloween*-style floating point-of-view puts death at arm's reach. Similarly unnerving editing adds a frighteningly jarring rhythm to sequences, as when quick jump cuts lurch spirits instantly towards the camera; or when a montage of stills cut to the sound of screaming obscures the full gory nature of a scene – and in obfuscating it only makes it worse.

Whispering Corridors fits alongside *The Craft* as a school-bound feminist horror that champions self-expression and support in both societal and artistic planes, with one character's grotesque but beautiful painting becoming a source for political upheaval and personal development. (The initials of the ghost "JJ" are etched on a class desk, and at one point when scouring a library, it's James Joyce's tale of personal awakening, *A Portrait of the Artist as a Young Man*, that is pulled out.) Creating art is an experience both positive and negative, and even if violently censored by the school at first, this art is what connects characters across classroom generations, flying in the face of their educators' passive but individualistic philosophy. Although you may not want to return to Jookran High for a while, for an exercise in smart – but still a bit silly – horror, *Whispering Corridors* gets top marks.

Opposite: Director Park Ki-hyung returned to the horror genre with 2003's 'tree ghost' chiller, *Acacia*.

Left: Student body. The high-school setting has served the *Whispering Corridors* franchise well, with six films released over 20 years. Here is an unfortunate victim from the fourth instalment, 2005's *Voice*.

SHIRI

쉬리

THE RISE OF THE KOREAN BLOCKBUSTER

With a landmark football match between North and South Korean teams looming, two secret agents are on the trail of a deadly assassin and a rogue military unit threatening Seoul with a devastating experimental explosive.

1999

Director: Kang Je-gyu

125 mins

Back in the early 1990s, Korean cinema wasn't even popular in Korea. Its market share at the domestic box office had sunk to a low of just 16% in 1993. Within a decade, though, that share had grown to almost half the overall admissions and box office takings, and in the years since it has become common for Korean films to command a dominating majority over Hollywood imports. That turnaround has been in part credited to a new generation of cineliterate filmmakers who rewrote the rule book, bending popular genres to suit new audiences – as we've seen in previous chapters on *Christmas in August* and *Whispering Corridors* – but a major sea change occurred in February 1999, with the release of the action thriller *Shiri*, the first of a new breed of Korean blockbuster.

Made for around $6 million – an indie budget in Hollywood money, but three times the average for a Korean film – this polished, precision-tooled popcorn flick attracted close to six million viewers in Korea, twenty times the average audience for a locally produced film. It was a bona fide blockbuster, and the most successful Korean film up to that point. To seal the deal that Hollywood supremacy was on the way out, it even sank the previous box office king: James Cameron's *Titanic*.

Born in 1962, director Kang Je-gyu grew up as a self-confessed "Hollywood kid". Yet, when he graduated from Seoul's Chung-Ang University in 1991, he was faced with the tough decision of either following his dream of making films, or pursuing a more stable career in the lucrative television or advertising sectors. He stuck with cinema, earning plaudits with his 1996 debut, the supernatural drama *Gingko Bed*, including a Best New Director prize at the Blue Dragon Film Awards (shared with Hong Sang-soo). Featuring rising star Han Suk-kyu and deploying extensive special effects in its telling of a romance across the centuries, *Gingko Bed* ended the year in second place at the Korean box office, pointing the way to what was to come.

That said, *Shiri* was unprecedented. Drawing inspiration from the '80s Hollywood action films that Kang grew up watching, as well as the best of Hong Kong cinema and more contemporary touchstones such as Michael Bay's *The Rock*, *Shiri* was a cultural phenomenon. The popularity of the kissing gourami fish that appear in the film reportedly went through the roof. And while it broke box office records at home, and took prizes such as the Blue Dragon Award for Best Director, it enjoyed rare international success, selling to 22 foreign territories,

Above: Face off. *Shiri* was Korea's all-guns-blazing attempt at an action blockbuster.

Above: "Nobody does it Better". Choi Min-sik, Oldboy himself, appears in Kang Je-gyu's film as a rogue North Korean agent.

Below: "Kiss kiss Bang Bang". Yu Jung-won and Lee Myung-hyun's romance bubbles away in a romantic and tragic style.

including France, North America and the UK (where it was packaged as part of the Tartan Films Asia Extreme label). Of particular note was the film's release in Japan, where it topped the charts on release and ended the year among the highest-grossing movies.

But for the Hollywood kid, topping *Titanic* held special meaning. Looking back at the release of *Shiri*, Kang Je-gyu told IndieWire: "Beating Hollywood films at the box office had been my dream for a long time. I grew up watching them and began to analyse the secrets of Hollywood

Above left: Fashion impossible. *Shiri* combines atomic threat with aquarium antics.

Above right: Licence to kill. Bringing North and South Korea together in bombastic fashion, *Shiri* results in a lot of blood.

Opposite: The spy who loved me. For all its action, *Shiri*'s success rested just as much on its melodrama.

filmmaking. I wanted to make a film that would entertain [Korean audiences] as much as Hollywood does... This film is the fruit of that labour: my dreams, thoughts and, well, even my suffering."

FURTHER VIEWING 👁

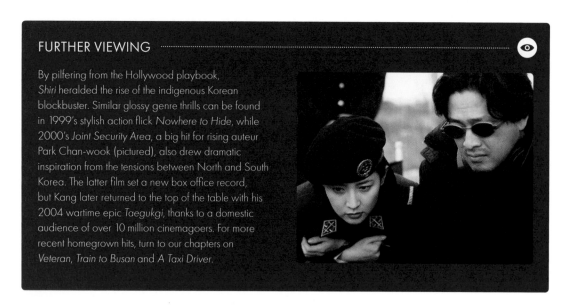

By pilfering from the Hollywood playbook, *Shiri* heralded the rise of the indigenous Korean blockbuster. Similar glossy genre thrills can be found in 1999's stylish action flick *Nowhere to Hide*, while 2000's *Joint Security Area*, a big hit for rising auteur Park Chan-wook (pictured), also drew dramatic inspiration from the tensions between North and South Korea. The latter film set a new box office record, but Kang later returned to the top of the table with his 2004 wartime epic *Taegukgi*, thanks to a domestic audience of over 10 million cinemagoers. For more recent homegrown hits, turn to our chapters on *Veteran*, *Train to Busan* and *A Taxi Driver*.

SHIRI – REVIEW

Shiri opens with military drums in the air, boots on the ground and a few glimpses of hotshot North Korean soldier Lee Bang-hee. The proceeding training montage sees Bang-hee execute a string of perfect headshots, burn up a family photo and kill a man for losing a gun-assembling race. This almost dialogue-free, instantly engaging opening very quickly circles, underlines and puts in bold just how much of a badass she is, and it's brilliant, ludicrous stuff. *Shiri* is first and foremost an extremely enjoyable action film – proudly wearing its Michael Bay and John Woo appreciation camp badges on its sleeve – but between the bullet spraying, bomb countdowns and telephone wire strangulations, there's also a murky, melancholy and romantic story that gives every gunshot even more heft.

A few years after the blazing intro, South Korean agents Yu Jung-won (Han Suk-kyu) and Lee Jang-gil (a cheery but trigger-happy Song Kang-Ho, showing his gift for flicking between light and dark, seen in many of his performances, especially *Parasite*) are on the hunt for the deadly Bang-hee, while carefully balancing their romantic lives and their investigative ones.

Where a less confident film might be eager to find the next set piece for the two to fire into, *Shiri* slows down after its relentless beginning, letting us learn about Jung-won and his fiancée Lee Myung-hyun (Kim Yun-jin), the owner of an aquarium store. Their relationship is sweet, the two sharing in the knowledge of types of fish, like the titular Shiri which swim in both North and South Korean rivers – Jung-won even populates his office with fish tanks from her store. Han and Kim's performances are melancholic and tender, providing far more intrigue and depth than an average potboiler action romance. But, after a few thundering taps into a weighty computer keyboard and some serious narrative whiplash, things start to go less swimmingly, especially when a potential terrorist bombing looms over the city, as well as an upcoming North vs South Korea soccer match.

Providing almost as much drama as South Korea's giant-killing run on their home turf during the 2002 World Cup, the film's action is comfortably clichéd, fun and a reminder of a lost art. In the last two decades, blockbuster action films have become the reliable mainstay of popular Western cinema – but, in between the quippy jokes and franchise scene setting, what do we actually see? Action might be the selling point, but the action itself is far too often just a grubby, weightless, computer-generated figure taking chunks out of another one of its kind. What's so refreshing about Shiri's attempt at action filmmaking at a high budget is the clarity and physicality of its action.

Though energetically captured, the film is never confusingly staged: we see cops with the aim of stormtroopers line up to get shot, back alleys get strewn with the tumbling detritus of any good foot chase, and of course, a shop full of fish tanks meets a shattering end. But at the final whistle, amid the debris, the film centres back to Jung-won and Myung-hyun, who share a look filled with tragedy, inevitability and love. Whether it's trying to unify a peninsula, track down a ruthless killer, or find a partner, *Shiri* shows that all of them are an upstream battle.

MY SASSY GIRL

엽기적인 그녀

SASS, ACTUALLY

College student Gyeon-woo encounters a drunk girl on the subway, and decides to help her find a motel for the night. Afterwards, their lives quickly become entangled – but this unpredictable girl is like no woman Gyeon-woo has ever met before.

2001

Director: Kwak Jae-yong

123 mins

"THE MOST BELOVED ROMANTIC COMEDY FROM ASIA,,,

my**sassy**girl

DIRECTOR'S CUT

,,,IS FINALLY AVAILABLE FOR THE FIRST TIME ON DVD"

If the Beatles' 'Yesterday' is the most covered piece of music of all time, *My Sassy Girl* is in with a shout of being the most covered, remade, or ripped off Korean film of all time. Adapted from the writing of Kim Ho-sik, whose true-life tales of his burgeoning relationship with a very atypical girlfriend were initially serialized online, *My Sassy Girl* was a huge hit at the Korean box office in 2001, selling close to 5 million tickets and ending the year second in the final tallies – beating out *Harry Potter and the Philosopher's Stone* and attracting double the audience of other Hollywood hits such as *Shrek* and *Pearl Harbor*.

Crucially, though, it travelled. It topped the box office in Hong Kong, and made a mint in Japan both at the box office and when it was released on DVD. And then came the remakes. Direct, unofficial or otherwise, *My Sassy Girl* was retold as a Japanese TV series, a straight-to-DVD Hollywood misfire, three Indian productions (in Hindi, Telugu and Malayalam), a record-breaking Nepali release, and the confusingly titled Chinese film *My Sassy Girl 2* (2010). It was such a hit in China that the 2016 sequel, *My New Sassy Girl*, was a co-production between Korean and Chinese companies, and paired up the male protagonist from the first film with his childhood love, who just so happens to be Chinese. While that film opened to a mixed response, the conceit was strong enough to inspire

Above: It girl. Jun Ji-hyun's live-wire performance as *My Sassy Girl*'s title character turned her into a star.

Below: Mysterious girl. Despite her forthright demeanour, the unnamed character has hidden depths of sorrow.

yet another version, 2017's Korean TV series *My Sassy Girl*, which transplanted the romantic pair into a period setting, with the female lead recast as more of a sassy princess.

None of these projects were as successful as the original, but it's easy to understand what made producers excited about getting their hands on the material. *My Sassy Girl* fits perfectly into the romantic comedy lineage of the time,

Above: New girl. Chinese actress-singer Victoria Song stars in the 2016 sequel, *My New Sassy Girl*.

Below: Carded. In one memorable scene, Gyeon-woo and "the girl" hit the town with their IDs in tow.

If you don't fancy falling down the rabbit hole of remakes of *My Sassy Girl* (and if you do, watch out for the dreadful American version), you can find many big-screen romances – tragic, melodramatic, comic – throughout Korean cinema, such as Kwak Jae-yong's follow-up, *The Classic* (2003), which swapped out the contemporary comedy style in favour of flashback-filled melodrama that cast Son Ye-jin (*The Truth Beneath*) in a dual role as both mother and daughter on parallel romantic journeys. Meanwhile, Jun Ji-hyun also starred in the timeslip romance *Il Mare* (remade in English as *The Lake House*). While Jun has made few films since *My Sassy Girl* catapulted her to stardom, many of them have been hits, ranging from Ryoo Seung-wan's thriller *The Berlin File* (2013) to a pair of huge blockbusters with director Choi Dong-hoon, the ensemble action-comedy *The Thieves* (2012) and period spy film *Assassination* (2015).

alongside the works of Nora Ephron (*Sleepless in Seattle; You've Got Mail*) and Richard Curtis (*Four Weddings and a Funeral; Notting Hill*), who made romance contemporary with modern, urban flourishes. *My Sassy Girl*, though, had an ace up its sleeve: its unnamed female lead, played with a compelling ferocity by Jun Ji-hyun. Writing for *Sight and Sound* in 2006, Grady Hendrix described the "fist-swinging girlfriend" as key to the film's appeal: "Director Kwak Jae-yong tweaked the genre's standard-issue quirky chick into a near-psychotic sadist whose sole expression of love is to humiliate and torture the object of her affections."

There's an unpredictable, once-seen-never-forgotten quality to the character, but for all the film's wildness, director Kwak Jae-yong is an old romantic at heart. Starting his career with the 1989 melodrama *Watercolour Painting in a Rainy Day*, he never drifted far away from love stories, whatever genre he turned his attention to. He says he learned that tendency from the films of Alfred Hitchcock, which found romance even within his most spectacular, suspenseful thrillers. Simply put, as he told the Korean Film Council, "a good film is a touching one".

Above: Second date. Writer-director Kwak-Jae-yong and actress Jun Ji-hyun reunited for the 2004 romantic drama *Windstruck*.

Right: Bad girl. The American remake of *My Sassy Girl*, starring Elisha Cuthbert, was released straight-to-DVD in 2008.

MY SASSY GIRL – REVIEW

"Wanna die?" It's not a catchphrase that immediately makes you think of a romcom, but Jun Ji-hyun's character (who is never given a name) in *My Sassy Girl* is particularly fond of it. Lacing her lacerations with dangerous, enthralling threat and buckets of charm, she issues death threats that are really love notes in camouflage, part of a unique dating artillery, in a unique film, that's totally to die for. After a hilarious, snowballing introduction in which student Gyeon-woo (Cha Tae-hyun) saves a drunk woman from a train collision, cleans up the vomit she projects onto the bald head (and toupee) of a passenger, gives her a piggyback to a hotel room and then gets arrested, he is not exactly enamoured. Suffice to say, this catastrophic union is their meet-cute, not a story from one of Gyeon-woo's "romantic comic books", but a delightfully puerile prelude to an emotional dance that is consistently surprising.

Although the title might suggest a possessiveness over his nameless girl, Gyeon-woo is not the least bit in control of Jun Ji-hyun's character: she's manic yes, but she is not a pixie dream girl. A tidal wave of soul-crushing eye rolls, provocations (like getting him out of class by saying he needs to pay for her abortion) and demands (like making him only ever order coffee at cafés), she is not in his control or built to his needs, but is her own wonderful explosion of passion and pain. Dressed consistently in red, brandishing her own form of social justice – whether securing train seats for the elderly (and then vomiting on them) or clearing prostitutes from restaurants – and leaving a trail of soju bottles in her wake, she is both femme fatale and boozing vigilante. She is still reeling from the untimely death of her previous partner, and her erratic behaviour and chaotic courtship with Gyeon-woo is a thoughtfully crafted exploration of grief, as much as it is a romance.

Imagining herself as a future screenwriter, she writes genre stories, portions of which appear throughout the film and which Kwak Jae-yong excels in directing. All featuring a character from "the future" played by Jun Ji-hyun, reflecting her character's suspension via grief, these gun-fu and martial arts scenes are surprisingly well crafted. Not just cheap gags (although one joke has dated badly), but expertly realized bites of spectacle, complete with cartwheeling, wall-running action. In the real-world setting, Kwak's deft direction of this sparkling and timeless story weaves between stirring, close-up intimacy and stylistic pomp, even squeezing in an all-timer dolly zoom perfectly capturing the combination of having a heart flutter and too much alcohol at the same time. "Koreans like melodramas," says Gyeon-woo at one point, and after *My Sassy Girl*, you can see why.

Above: Meet cute. Our unlikely couple initially cross paths after Gyeon-woo finds "the girl" hopelessly drunk, and escorts her to the safety of a hotel room.

Above: Coffee date. Offended by Gyeon-woo's unsophisticated choice of drink, the girl forces him to order a more grown-up kind of beverage.

WAIKIKI BROTHERS

와이키키 브라더스

BAND ON THE RUN

After years on the road, the touring band Waikiki Brothers hits rock bottom and takes a residency playing nightly gigs at a hotel in frontman Sung-woo's hometown. There, he reconnects with friends, mentors and former flames, contemplating the future and looking back on a life dedicated to a musical career that never took off.

2001

Director: Yim Soon-rye

109 mins

제2회 전주국제영화제 개막작

와이키키 브라더스

WAIKIKI BROTHERS

막다른 길… 그러나 되돌아갈 수 있다는 희망

임순례 감독 작품

이 얼 · 황정민 · 박원상 · 오지혜 · 류승범 · 오광록 특별출연 김영수

〈공동경비구역JSA〉의 명필름 2001년 첫 작품

제작 이 은 | 부제작 이우정 | 제작투자 석동준 | 촬영 최지열 | 조명 임재영 | 미술 오상만 | 편집 김상범 | 음악 최순식 · 김민우 | 사운드 김석원 | 동시녹음 한철희 | 소품 이종국
의상 한혜숙 · 홍정희 | 분장 이부남 | 헤어 손은주 | 현장사진 김진원 | 포스터사진 오형근 | 광고디자인 임근영 | 제작팀장 신 철 | 조감독 조승희 | 국내마케팅책임 박재현 | 해외마케팅 조은정 | 해외세일즈 Paul Yi

제작 명필름 제공 CJ Entertainment | www.myungfilm.com | www.waikikibrothers.com

OB라거 Cass Green

1996 was a key year for Korean cinema. It saw the launch of the Busan International Film Festival, which has become one of Asia's leading film festivals, and an important showcase for the country's films and filmmakers. The inaugural year featured high-profile debuts from three promising directors: Hong Sang-soo (*The Day a Pig Fell into the Well*), Kim Ki-duk (*Crocodile*), and Yim Soon-rye, whose first film, *Three Friends*, made her only the seventh female filmmaker in Korean cinema history.

Born in 1961, Yim grew up as a passionate reader, devouring the work of William Shakespeare, Leo Tolstoy, Fyodor Dostoevsky and Johann Wolfgang von Goethe, and later studied at Hanyang University's English Department. There, she discovered French cinema, specifically the work of director Bertrand Tavernier, and travelled to Paris for graduate school – a move partly influenced by the hope that she could spend her days at the Cinémathèque Française. By her calculations, she saw over a thousand films during her time in Paris, sometimes watching up to three or four a day. Her master's thesis was a study of the work of Japanese director Kenji Mizoguchi, but her extracurricular viewing covered everything from Akira Kurosawa, Yasujirō Ozu and Andrei Tarkovsky to Emil Kusturica, Theo Angelopoulos and Krzysztof Kieślowski.

Back in Korea, Yim pursued a career in film but didn't follow the standard route into the industry, where film graduates would apprentice on studio productions on their way to the director's chair. Instead, she made the short film *Promenade in the Rain*, which won a prize at the Seoul Short Film Festival. Sensing an opportunity, she secured financing for a debut feature from the festival's sponsors, Samsung Entertainment Group. *Three Friends* was made on a tight budget, for less than half of the cost of the average Korean film of the time.

Yim's second feature, *Waikiki Brothers*, arrived towards the end of 2001. Neither a conventional teen movie or music film, *Waikiki Brothers* follows the existential crisis of a musician as his prospects of fronting a successful band are on the wane. The film was Yim's exploration of the sometimes harsh realities of adulthood. As she told Lee Yoo-ran, "no one lives just as they had dreamed in their youth."

Yim followed *Waikiki Brothers* with a documentary, *Keeping the Vision Alive: Women in Korean Filmmaking*, which looked back to the pioneering careers of directors such as Park Nom-ok (*The Widow*) and forward to a new generation of female filmmakers. As one of the leading female directors in recent Korean cinema history, Yim sees her responsibilities as lying just as much behind the scenes

as on the big screen, including supporting the Centre for Gender Equality in Korean Film, an organization founded in 2020 in the wake of #MeToo and #TimesUp.

Unlike some of her contemporaries, who live and breathe cinema even in their middle age – such as Hong Sang-soo, who claimed in an interview with Huh Moon-young that outside of directing he has no hobbies apart from drinking – Yim is more than just a filmmaker or a cinephile. She is also a pescetarian, a lover of nature and an animal rights advocate. "Cinema is not everything in my life," she told Lee Yoo-ran. "I don't feel I have to make films no matter what – I am more interested in life itself."

FURTHER VIEWING 👁

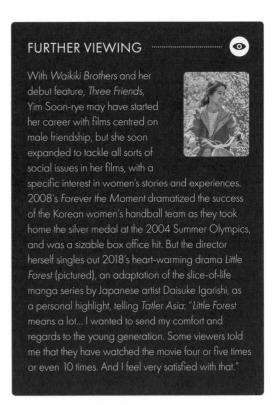

With *Waikiki Brothers* and her debut feature, *Three Friends*, Yim Soon-rye may have started her career with films centred on male friendship, but she soon expanded to tackle all sorts of social issues in her films, with a specific interest in women's stories and experiences. 2008's *Forever the Moment* dramatized the success of the Korean women's handball team as they took home the silver medal at the 2004 Summer Olympics, and was a sizable box office hit. But the director herself singles out 2018's heart-warming drama *Little Forest* (pictured), an adaptation of the slice-of-life manga series by Japanese artist Daisuke Igarishi, as a personal highlight, telling *Tatler Asia*: "*Little Forest* means a lot... I wanted to send my comfort and regards to the young generation. Some viewers told me that they have watched the movie four or five times or even 10 times. And I feel very satisfied with that."

WAIKIKI BROTHERS – REVIEW

The story of musicians in film often chimes to a familiar collection of melodies. There's the glittery, driving scales of biopics like *Rocketman* or *Elvis*, the crescendos and crashes of fame in *A Star is Born*, the underdog grind of *Anvil: The Story of Anvil* or the jukebox joys of musical discovery in *School of Rock* – all with recognizable beats, ready to be covered, again and again. These are films where the road to success is not always straight; it climbs and dips, has the odd pothole in, but eventually reaches its destination. In *Waikiki Brothers*, the titular band don't travel on one of those roads, they're on a roundabout.

"The Beatles of night clubs" is their ironic introduction. But there's no swarming crowds, screeching fans or even a merch table, and there is certainly no Waikiki-mania. This is the story of a jobbing band, who share rooms but are painfully lonely, and whose role is to play in the background, at just the right volume for dancing, and not so loud as to disrupt dinner. Unceremoniously presented, but beautifully performed, passionate sax solos, intricate guitar licks and soulful, romantic crooning float into the rafters of quarter-empty venues, and their disinterested clientele. They are skilled musicians, passionate about rock and roll, but out of step with their time. Set at the turn of the 21st century, the analogue Waikiki Brothers know that their biggest rivals aren't other bands, they're synthesizers, drum machines and karaoke. After a conveyor belt of bad gigs, Sung-woo (Lee Eol) gets dragged into a karaoke booth by some friends from his youth, and the empty orchestra transports us to the formation of his band.

Innocent, excitable and emotional, Sung-woo and his band brim with adolescent expectation, both in music and romance, but every line about their world-conquering dreams is tragically underscored by their future, isolated reality. Across time, their actions start to circulate: a teen's hilarious flaming amplifier escapade is mirrored in an alcoholic's unintentional arson; the joy of skinny-dipping with friends becomes the melancholy memory of a tired musician, forced to strip by their client. Leading the band, and the film, Lee

Opposite top: Plastic oh no band. Reduced to performing in off-season hotels, the Waikiki Brothers realize they'll never achieve their dream of pop-star success.

Above: Yesterday. A flashback to the group's first rehearsals and performances captures a youthful optimism they lost over time.

Eol gives a remarkable performance, both frontman and spectre: his tired eyes and floating gait haunt the film, providing one of the most authentic and relatable representations of burnout available.

There's a ghostliness to the film's settings as well, capturing the strange liminality of the working musician's shifts. Performing at night, they drift through their days, when the streets seem as empty as some of their dance floors and the interiors of different venues all start to look the same, mulching day, night, performance and person together.

The slow fracturing of the band feels inevitable, but there's no bust-up that seals their fate, just the attrition of reality, and what makes it so sad to watch is that Waikiki Brothers are a great band! They have talent and, like the Coen brothers' Llewyn Davis, they would have been recognized in another place, or another time, and become stars. Despite the pain, and the boredom, they keep taking to the stage even when there is the chance of an exit route. Masochistic, artistic or so wrecked by a gig economy that they have nothing else they can do, the lure, and the trap, of the stage endures.

TAKE CARE OF MY CAT

고양이를 부탁해

GIRL FRIENDS

After graduating high school, five young
women from the port town of Incheon make
their first tentative steps into adulthood.
As they enter the working world, their once
tight-knit friendship starts to fray.

2001

Director: Jeong Jae-eun

112 mins

While commercial Korean cinema was on the rise, a new generation of female filmmakers was making their mark in the margins. *Take Care of My Cat*, the first film from a female director to have a big-screen release in almost three years, may not have bothered the box office in October 2001, but it was widely acclaimed both at home and abroad, and has been a cult favourite ever since.

Born in 1969, director Jeong Jae-eun studied at the Korean National University of the Arts, and was part of the film department's first graduating class after it opened in 1995. In her academic study *Women's Cinema, World Cinema*, Patricia White cites the boom of film schools as a major turning point for the fortunes of female filmmakers in Korea. Previously, budding directors had to prove themselves over lengthy apprenticeships as assistants, but now, as director Helen Lee told White, women could "train in film school, write commercially viable scripts, make a short to prove their directorial ability, and get [funding]".

Jeong cut her teeth on a series of short films, many of which focused on the interior lives of girls and young women, including *Girls' Night Out* and *Yu-jin's Secret Code*, the latter of which won the Grand Prize for short

films at the Seoul International Women's Film Festival in 1999. Following this, she had the opportunity to develop her feature debut with producer Oh Ki-min (*Whispering Corridors*), who had set up his own production company, Masulpiri Pictures. There, *Take Care of My Cat* shared the slate with Kim Jee-woon's horror flick *A Tale of Two Sisters*.

In conversation with FilmFestivals.com, Jeung Jae-eun explained that her aim with this ensemble feature was "to focus on normal, usual friendships and relationships and the way they evolve, develop." A director's statement quoted by Darcy Paquet on his indispensable website KoreanFilm.org goes further: "There have been no movies in the past that have depicted well how young Korean women think, how they play and what they worry about. I hope that this film can give audiences a sense of what young Korean women are like and how beautiful they are."

While it wasn't a blockbuster on release, *Take Care of My Cat* took home its fair share of prizes, for Jeong Jae-eun's direction as well as the performances from rising stars Bae Doona and Lee Yo-won. Festival appearances in Busan, Rotterdam, Berlin, Edinburgh, Toronto and Hong Kong, and theatrical releases in Japan, the United Kingdom and the United States gave the film an international profile. Back home, it became known as a "commercial orphan", but fans and supporters of the film stepped in. Grassroots screenings were organized in both Incheon and Seoul, the latter as part of a series celebrating independent "non-commercial" releases, bearing the catchy title WaRaNaGo. The name was formed from the first syllables of the titles of the films in the line-up, the others being Yim Soon-rye's *Waikiki Brothers*, Jang Hyeon-su's *Raybang* and Moon Seung-wook's *Nabi*.

However, this cat had a long tail. A 20th-anniversary restoration premiered, very appropriately, at the Seoul International Women's Festival in 2021, where the film was heralded as a "provocative but light-hearted feminist pleasure", and its influence continues to be felt. *Take Care of My Cat* was highlighted by screenwriter Chung Seo-kyung (*Decision to Leave*, *The Handmaiden*) as a film that made her want to make movies herself, and she told *Sight and Sound* in 2022: "Even watching it now, the film has lost none of its charm."

Left: Feline friends. The eponymous cat becomes a tie that binds together the film's characters as they start to grow apart.

Opposite top: Girl gang. *Take Care of My Cat*'s ensemble is a snapshot of young womanhood in turn-of-the-millennium Korea.

FURTHER VIEWING

While Jeong Jae-eun (pictured) has made a couple of features since *Take Care of My Cat* (including 2005's *The Aggressives* and 2017's *Butterfly Sleep*), she has found a new lease of creative life as a documentary filmmaker, focusing on the intersection between architecture and urban life, from *Talking Architect* (2012) and *Ecology in Concrete* (2017) to *Cats' Apartment* (2020), which studied a community of cats living in an abandoned apartment block that had been marked for demolition. Meanwhile, Bae Doona has gone on to enjoy a successful career in films of all sizes, including Bong Joon-ho's blockbuster *The Host*, Park Chan-wook's cult favourite *Sympathy*

for *Mr. Vengeance*, and July Jung's low-budget indie drama *A Girl at My Door*. She has also become one of the most recognizable Korean stars on the world stage, after starring roles in Japanese films such as the high-school band comedy *Linda Linda Linda* and Hirokazu Kore-eda's offbeat drama *Air Doll*, and becoming a key company player for the Wachowskis in *Jupiter Ascending*, *Cloud Atlas* and *Sense8*.

Above: Hold the phone. *Take Care of My Cat*'s focus on cell phones and texting heralded the rise of a new, tech-savvy generation.

Below: Actress Bae Doona is one of Korea's most engaging stars, as covered later in this book in *The Girl at My Door*.

TAKE CARE OF MY CAT – REVIEW

Above: Shin Hye-ju, played by Lee Yo-won, is the group's most upwardly-mobile member, aspiring to live a big-city life with a corporate job.

A new millennium film for the new millennial filmgoer, *Take Care of My Cat* is a tenderly observed but never syrupy portrait of the tightening and splintering nature of early adult friendships. Balancing delicate interpersonal detailing with sharp societal critique, Jeong Jae-eun's film reveals the fraying pettiness that can form beyond the bubble of school years, and the bureaucratic cruelty wielded to those less fortunate. It is, however, also a tremendously warm film, one that settles viewers into the rhythms of a friendship, its quirks and its cracks, and the confusing spinning compass of twenty-something life choices.

Beginning with a black tile, a zoom out reveals a map of the Earth made up of these tiles, the map a decoration in the demanding office of Hae-joo (Lee Yo-won), a high-school graduate who has thrown herself into her work and made it her world. Hye-ju's closest friends are Tae-hee (Bae Doona), who works at her family's sauna and dreams of escaping her conformist family, independent twins Lee Eun-sil and Lee Eun-ju, who sell their own jewellery, and Ji-young (Ok Ji-young), who's unemployed and living with her grandparents in a house whose roof is near collapse. At a birthday party Ji-young gifts Hye-ju a stray kitten. Unwanted, it migrates between the group, tying them together – the sisterhood of the travelling cat.

Even when they're apart, the friends are kept together by their cell phones (by 2001 already a fixture in every pocket and bag), either joined by split-screen calls or creatively deployed on-screen texting. Jeong knows that reading a text on a phone screen isn't the most dynamic or emotional way of using screen time, so typed words appear on furniture and windows, not just making a more interesting visual experience but showing how the technology has become a part of the landscape itself. As well as this engaged use, phones are glared at and weaponized, sitting heavy in the hand, Jeong understanding the power of the cell phone to be both a tool for freedom and an anchor of anxiety.

The challenges of the group mutate from the task of simply getting everyone together, to the red tape of finding employment without the right qualifications or privileged access, to grief, abandonment and juvenile detention. The wealth divide, especially between workaholic Hae-joo and jobless Ji-young, eventually causes rifts in the group and Ji-young starts to fall through the cracks of her friends, and of society. Regularly contrasting the frail, compact housing of Ji-young's Incheon, to Hae-joo's sleek Seoul, Jeong's future documentary direction is tested here, her interest in both lifestyle and architecture on show.

A predecessor to female-led millennial malaise favourites like *Frances Ha*, *The Worst Person in the World* and *Girls*, *Take Care of My Cat* is presented with a freewheeling, accessible style that smoothly wanders into complexity and a rich wisdom that feels resonant today. Although there might be love between the women, they're smart enough to know when their time as a unit is over, like the familiar, but no less emotional, end to a tragic romance. A joyous final shot turns the interiority of the story outwards, turning the possibilities of the world into a gateway, not the decoration of an office. It is followed by the curious title card of "Good Bye", reassuring us that, despite their flaws, this is not for these loveable characters "The End".

SAVE THE GREEN PLANET!

고양이를 부탁해

PSEUDO SUPERHERO

Convinced that the Earth is in imminent danger and only he can save it, an eccentric loner kidnaps the head of a pharmaceutical company – a member, he believes, of an invading alien race.

2003
Director: Jang Joon-hwan
118 mins

Above: Wet suit. With his eccentric uniform, unorthodox methods, and obsessive drive, Byeong-gu is a peculiar parody of the world-saving hero.

Below: Deep heat after me... Byeong-gu's use of roll-on liquid painkiller as an interrogation device goes against all sound medical advice.

To many film fans, Korean cinema is synonymous with films that blend and bend genres – but *Save the Green Planet!* is in a class of its own. Part sci-fi, part slapstick comedy, part abduction thriller, part superhero spoof, all adding up to the kind of *sui generis* curiosity that is few and far between in commercial cinema. And yet first-time director Jang Joon-hwan somehow got it made. And not only that, it travelled, slipping perfectly into Tartan Video's Asia Extreme label on its release in the UK.

Born in 1970 in the small city of Jeonju in Jeolla Province, Jang grew up loving movies – mostly, by his own admission, as a way of avoiding studying. He recalls spending weekends at a local cinema that programmed double bills throughout the day, and even screened imported Hong Kong films and Hollywood B-movies on video out of hours. The management had a relaxed approach to age restrictions, so Jang was able to sneak into films that he was definitely too young to see, such as *The Texas Chain Saw Massacre* (1974) and the Shaw Brothers' women-in-prison exploitation flick *The Bamboo House of Dolls* (1973). Hollywood films made up the majority of his diet, with favourites ranging from *Terms of Endearment* (1983) and the films of Woody Allen, to *Blade Runner* (1982) and *The Silence of the Lambs* (1991), to the broad popcorn comedy of *Three Amigos* (1985).

But the first film he saw at the cinema left a deep impression: Richard Donner's comic-book epic, *Superman: The Movie* (1978). Decades later, *Save the Green Planet!* would play with the superhero mythos, turning the archetype inside out and, as Jang told the Korean Film Council, depicting "a hero suffering from an obsession . . . to save the Earth." This conceit was married to two other ideas inspired, both directly and indirectly, by Hollywood cinema. Upon seeing the Stephen King adaptation *Misery* (1990), Jang was disappointed that the film didn't sufficiently explore the inner workings of Kathy Bates' crazed kidnapper, Annie Wilkes, so he wanted to flesh out such a character of his own. Then, he happened upon a report about an online community which believed that film star and heartthrob Leonardo DiCaprio was, in fact, an alien taking over the Earth by seducing the planet's women.

This mix of film genres and references suggests something of Jang's taste. However, unlike many filmmakers of his generation, he shies away from calling himself a film fan or cinephile. This is in stark contrast to the likes of two of his early collaborators, Ryoo Seung-wan and Bong Joon-ho, the latter his classmate at the Korean Academy of Film Arts. Jang served as cinematographer on Ryoo's short film *Transmutated Head* (1996) and was lighting technician for

FURTHER VIEWING 👁

After his wild, unclassifiable debut proved to be a box office disappointment, Jang Joon-hwan (pictured) didn't make another feature for a decade, returning in a mellower, more commercially viable mode with the violent action-thriller *Hwayi: A Monster Boy* (2013) and the political thriller *1987: When the Day Comes* (2017), which was a huge hit both with critics and at the box office, selling over 7 million tickets. For more idiosyncratic, genre-blending Korean cinema of the period, try the crime comedy *Attack the Gas Station* (1999), Bong Joon-ho's quirky debut, *Barking Dogs Never Bite* (1999), and the horror-drama *Spider Forest* (2003).

Bong's *Incoherence* (1994), while Bong shot and co-edited Jang's graduate project, *2001 Imagine* (1994).

Yet even in this blossoming generation of directors with strong, distinctive visions, *Save the Green Planet!* stuck out. "He has created a peculiar world," notes critic Choi Eun-young, "the likes of which are difficult to find either before or after." Jang himself gives it a different spin, telling the Korean Film Council: "Since I was a child, I have been very absent-minded . . . it appears that I have had a lot of wild ideas."

Above: Bee movie. Byeong-gu's bee colony comes to the rescue when a snooping detective comes calling.

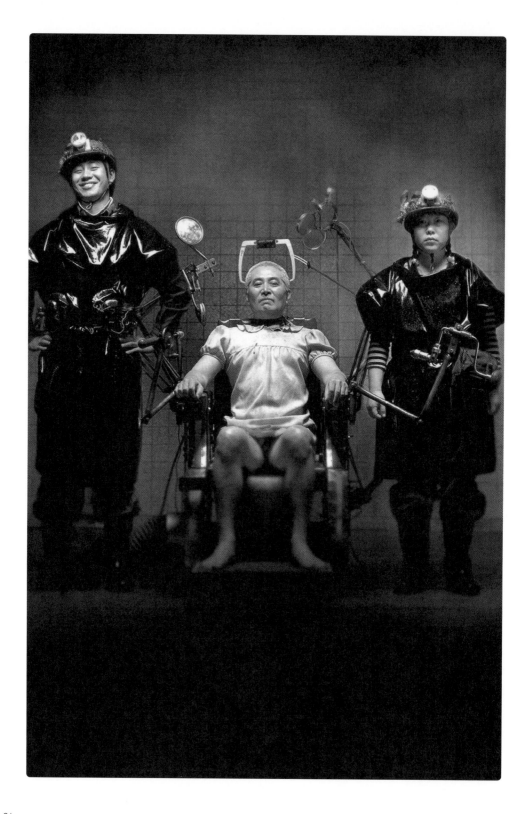

SAVE THE GREEN PLANET! – REVIEW

A reverse superhero story, told from the perspective of a villain, not the caped crusader, who needs to save the world. Two decades on from the release of *Save the Green Planet!*, that's the kind of pitch which ends up being a key cog in the content machine of a comic-book movie corporation looking for fresh ideas. In 2003, it was a flop. Jang Joon-hwan's wild cinematic universe is a genre-smashing triumph of the strange, assembling wildly different modes to tell a story that is both simple, human tragedy and planet-ending event.

With tinfoil hats firmly strapped on, the film's "heroes" are Byeong-gu, a disturbed beekeeper and mannequin builder (a fantastic professional combination to earmark eeriness) and his circus-performer partner Su-ni. The two begin the film by kidnapping pharmaceutical executive Kang Man-shik, fearing that he might be an alien about to launch an attack against Planet Earth – and who is coincidentally also Byeong-gu's ex-boss. Strapping

him into a nightmarish dentist's chair crossed with a commode in Byeong-gu's grimy, green-tinted basement, they then start their interrogation. Initially unfolding like a screwball Gilliam-esque sci-fi, with its wide angles, harsh lighting, spidery metal contraptions and pervading paranoia, Jang's confident filmmaking swiftly and nimbly pivots between styles.

As Kang (who may not even be the first victim) is tortured to increasingly grisly lengths, a police investigation runs alongside, which Jang directs with cool aplomb. Dexterously shifting to a slick investigative drama, the more grounded style helps to reframe Byeong-gu's actions as the frenzied, not vigilante, acts that they are. When one detective gets too close to the truth, he ends up covered in sugar water, is attacked by bees and then falls off a cliff – the results shown in gruesome detail. Jang uses the film to show off his gore credentials, as well as his procedural ones.

Jang cites the lack of Annie Wilkes' characterization in *Misery* as an inspiration to the deranged Byeong-gu, whose moving backstory – in which he's a victim of abuse, then himself becomes violent, and his mother is severely injured at Kang's factory and rendered comatose – explains his psychosis as a bloody escape fantasy. Ironically Sun-i, his partner in crime, isn't given the same treatment, her character entirely shaped by her quirks of tightrope walking, liking dolls and loving Byeong-gu.

An English-language remake, from acclaimed director Ari Aster, who along with producer Lars Knudsen described the original as one of the "most remarkable films to come out of South Korea", is currently on the cards. Having together explored conspiratorial organisations, cycles of violence and buckets of gore in *Hereditary* and *Midsommar*, they're now interested in retelling Jang's story for the "mess of the world today", whether the aliens are real or not.

Opposite: Chair man. Baek Yoon-sik won several high-profile awards for his turn as the kidnapped CEO Kang Man-shik.

Above: High-wire act. One of *Save the Green Planet*'s most bizarre characters is Byeong-gu's girlfriend-accomplice, Sun-i, who moonlights as a circus performer.

A TALE OF TWO SISTERS

장화, 홍련

HOUSE ON HAUNTED HILL

Loosely based on the Korean folktale "Janghwa Hongryeon jeon", this haunted house horror sees a teenage girl return from a mental institution to be reunited with her sister and stepmother, only to then have to deal with disturbing events back home.

2003

Director: Kim Jee-woon

114 mins

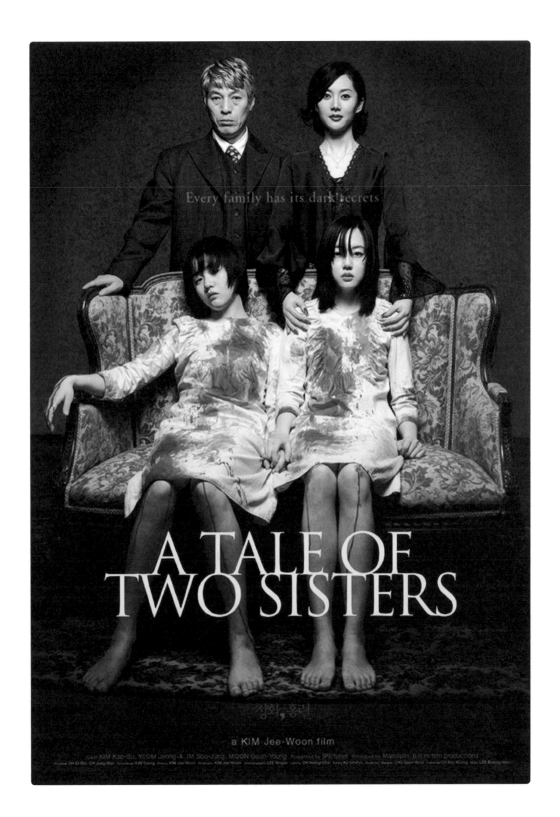

Before he became one of Korea's most exciting and eclectic filmmakers, Kim Jee-woon was a self-described dropout. As he tells it, "the longest time I ever spent at a job in my life was when I was a slacker" – a full decade, by his count. In those years through his twenties and into his thirties he lived with his parents, took on odd jobs in theatre and film, and lacked any direction whatsoever. "I didn't have any desire for accomplishment," he wrote in the biographical essay "Living as a Film Director".

What he did have, though, was a deep love of cinema that had been fostered at a young age. His father was an avid film fan with a vast knowledge of Hollywood trivia, and films offered one of the few ways that young Kim could connect with his dad. His other passion was drawing, and these were the two lights that led him through what by all accounts was a difficult and lonely childhood. Kim recounts that a local cinema would put up film posters outside their house in exchange for free tickets, which he would take for himself and use to watch whatever was playing. He was dazzled by the range of genres on offer, from romances to comedies, spy thrillers to monster movies, sci-fi to horror. And he watched it all.

By the time he started school, he was already in the habit of assigning star ratings to films, and his obsession grew from there, never distinguishing between art or commercial cinema, or high- and lowbrow. When listing his favourite films, he's likely to place *Terminator 2: Judgment Day* (1991) and *Ed Wood* (1994) alongside cinephile favourites such as Andrei Tarkovsky's *Mirror* (1975) and Ingmar Berman's *The Virgin Spring* (1960). As a young adult, he trawled video stores for illegal copies of films unreleased in Korea, amassed a collection of LaserDiscs, and attended screenings at the French Cultural Centre. Looking back, he described the films he watched in these impressionable years as "a tsunami of masterpieces", from *Midnight Express* (1978) and *A*

Clockwork Orange (1971) to *Akira* (1988) and *Ghost in the Shell* (1995) to the work of French masters Jean-Luc Godard, Jean-Pierre Melville, François Truffaut and René Clément. During his slacker phase, he saved up for a five-month trip to Europe, most of which he spent in Paris, where he regularly visited the Cinémathèque Française and hoovered up a season of films billed as 100 Masterpieces of World Cinema. By his count, he saw 110 films in his three-month stay in the city.

"All a director needs is to have a fantasy to create another world," Kim once told the Korean Film Council. It probably helps that he's quite the storyteller, especially when it comes to events in his own life. Take it with a pinch of salt, but the yarn goes that he fully embraced cinema as a career after two events: being dumped by his girlfriend and crashing his car. "I needed to pay for repairs," he told film critic Kim Hyung-seok, "but I didn't have any money... At that time, the only way I was going to make a lot of money was robbing a bank or writing a script. I didn't feel like putting my life on the line robbing a bank, so that was out, and so I came to write a script for the first time." Kim won scriptwriting competitions held by the film magazines *Première* and *Cine21*, giving rise to another tall tale he likes to weave. One day, he ordered ramen in a restaurant, and rather than carrying the bowl on a tray, the waitress served his meal resting on an issue of *Cine21* that advertised the competition. The script he submitted would become his directorial debut, *The Quiet Family*, which was released in 1998 when he was 33, and proved to be a

Above: Su-mi and Su-yeon divided by "that woman", stepmother Eun-joo.

Left: Kim Kap-soo as Bae Moo-hyeon, the father caught in the maternal melodrama.

Opposite top: Full of twists, turns and gnarly moments, Kim Jee-woon's film will floor some faint-hearted audiences.

KOREAN DIRECTORS IN THE UNITED STATES

As Korean cinema's international standing flourished, its leading filmmakers have been tempted to travel across the Pacific and make English-language films in Hollywood. Kim Jee-woon (pictured) made the leap with 2013's *The Last Stand*, an explosive if inessential action flick that gave Arnold Schwarzenegger his first leading role following his tenure as Governor of California. In the same year, Park Chan-wook fared better with the charged psychological thriller *Stoker*, and later won acclaim for the BBC adaptation of John le Carrè's spy thriller *The Little Drummer Girl*, starring Florence Pugh. Bong Joon-ho, too, was courted by Western producers for projects ranging from *13 Assassins* (2010) to what eventually became the Will

Smith vehicle *Hancock* (2008), but he has always preferred to follow his own path: even the international productions *Snowpiercer* (2013) and *Okja* (2017) kept one foot firmly planted in the Korean film industry.

key release for a new generation of Korean filmmakers shaking up the industry – although, unlike his peers, Kim stood out as having no training or significant hands-on experience. If you take him at his word, he had never even held a camcorder before he directed his first film.

"I didn't follow the formula of others," he told Kim Hyung-seok, "I entered this road through a slightly special course of life. The roads that you stumble upon when you've lost your way are how maps are made." A lifetime spent drinking deeply from the well of cinema prepared Kim for the shift from his slacker phase to his filmmaker phase. The films poured out of him, both features and shorts, as he hopped from genre to genre with every new project. 2003's *A Tale of Two Sisters* was his first dip into horror, and was a hit at the Korean box office in a year that also saw major works from Park Chan-wook (*Oldboy*) and Bong Joon-ho (*Memories of Murder*). Riding a wave of interest in Asian horror in the early 2000s, the film was released in the United States and the United Kingdom, where it perfectly suited Tartan Film's Asia Extreme library.

FURTHER VIEWING

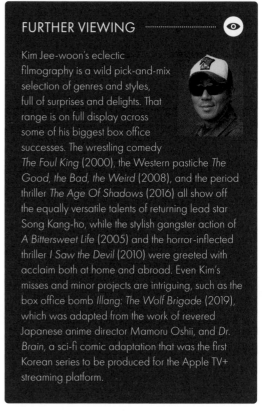

Kim Jee-woon's eclectic filmography is a wild pick-and-mix selection of genres and styles, full of surprises and delights. That range is on full display across some of his biggest box office successes. The wrestling comedy *The Foul King* (2000), the Western pastiche *The Good, the Bad, the Weird* (2008), and the period thriller *The Age Of Shadows* (2016) all show off the equally versatile talents of returning lead star Song Kang-ho, while the stylish gangster action of *A Bittersweet Life* (2005) and the horror-inflected thriller *I Saw the Devil* (2010) were greeted with acclaim both at home and abroad. Even Kim's misses and minor projects are intriguing, such as the box office bomb *Illang: The Wolf Brigade* (2019), which was adapted from the work of revered Japanese anime director Mamoru Oshii, and *Dr. Brain*, a sci-fi comic adaptation that was the first Korean series to be produced for the Apple TV+ streaming platform.

A TALE OF TWO SISTERS – REVIEW

Before this book, the writers wrote one all about Japanese animation legends Studio Ghibli. So there's something familiar about an early scene in this film, featuring two sisters clambered into a car with their dad and driving out to a remote, perhaps haunted, house in the countryside. For a short moment, it seems inspired by Hayao Miyazaki's heartening adventure *My Neighbour Totoro*. There, the girls enter their ghostly home, hurtle around corners screaming spirits away and embrace their fantastical adventure with glee. Here, though, the girls do not have such a nice time. In fact, when director Jordan Peele was preparing actress Lupita Nyong'o for his fiercely intense film *Us*, to get her dialled in for her perfectly terrifying performance, he gave her a list of films to watch; it included the likes of *The Shining*, *The Babadook*, *It Follows* and Kim Jee-woon's *A Tale of Two Sisters*.

Su-mi has recently spent some time in a mental institution, and when she arrives with her sister Su-yeon at their house, the air is thick with animosity towards their waiting stepmother Eun-joo. Covered in luxurious, detailed wallpaper, antique wooden fixtures and ornate lighting, the mansion feels more like an exhibit, prepared for visitation and observation. (For more gloriously designed, English country style in Korea, check out Park Chan-wook's *The Handmaiden*.) The sisters stare, grimace and stew in silence the way that only teenagers can. Their new rural mansion may have once been a home but now leaves us wondering whether Su-mi has moved from one prison to another.

At night, the house's secrets start to be teased, in nail-biting fashion. Resurrecting the terror of sleepless childhood nights, Kim's agonizingly extended takes remind viewers of the simple fears of creaking doors, unfamiliar footsteps, scary cupboards – and the blanket that can be pulled up as a shield. Moving the camera at a glacial speed, the house becomes a space where the terrors of a broken family, or of the supernatural, could hide behind every wall, the exacting direction drawing tension from every moment.

The relationship between Su-mi and Eun-joo (or, as bitterly named by the sisters, "that woman") has a curious, gnarled dynamic, whose shape is only explained in the closing moments of the film, as the nature of their biological mother's departure comes to light. At points the gothic home, looming grief and emotional distance makes the film feel like a maternal *Rebecca*, while the scares, which gradually move from supernatural to harsh, human abuse, shift the identity of the defined monster, similarly to Guillermo del Toro's brand of horror. Complementing the balance of tight terror and melodrama is the score by Lee Byung-woo (who would go on to work on Bong Joon-ho's *The Host* and *Mother*), its swelling strings and warm plucked guitar offsetting the unease with surprising romance.

Compared to the quiet kids, Eun-joo talks and talks, in an attempt to fill the deathly silence. Yum Jung-ah's performance is superb, straddling fear and hatred, her true feelings towards her stepchildren never fully readable. At an incredibly awkward dinner party – in which a distinctly European meal adds to the peculiarity – her motormouth starts to choke, or is perhaps possessed, making for one of the film's most rattling scenes.

At first a ghost story, *A Tale of Two Sisters* gradually strips away its fantastical elements to focus on domestic horror. Recurring imagery of birdcages, the use of kitchens as scare locations, and a sense of consistent filial and spousal servitude shows the patriarchal structure of the house, with Su-mi forcing against and Eun-joo prying her way in, by any morbid means. In the final scenes, unreliable psychological states, ghosts and memories merge to dole out thrilling, twisting revelations, decorating events in a far crueller palette. It's beautifully realized, mercilessly cruel viewing, and you might need to watch *My Neighbour Totoro* again afterwards just to recover.

Opposite top: Beautifully designed, stepmother Eun-joo's new home is covered in stunning wallpaper and ornamentation.

Opposite bottom: Sister company. The film explores the intense bond between sisters, and the pain of separation.

OLDBOY

올드보이

KOREA EXTREME

In 1988, Oh Dae-su was kidnapped and imprisoned for 15 years. After he is mysteriously released, he sets out to find his estranged daughter, and track down his captors.

2003
Director: Park Chan-wook
120 mins

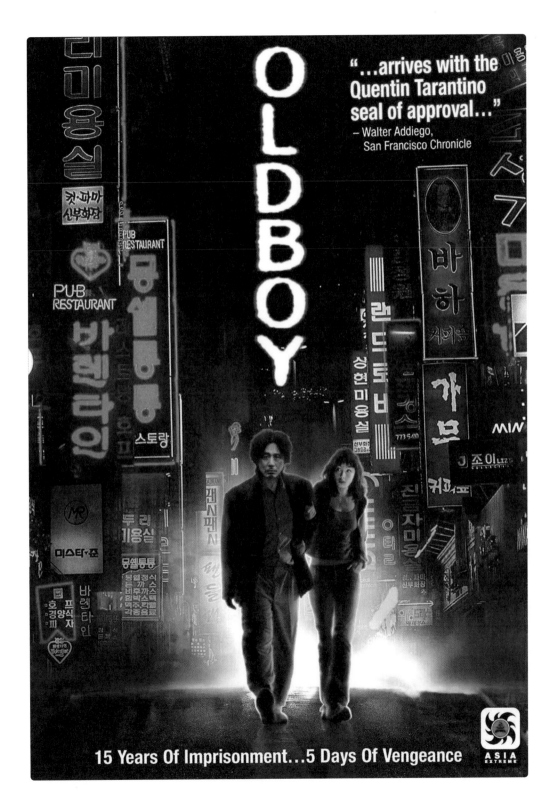

"No doubt about it, *Oldboy* is all about extremity," opened a review that seems in retrospect rather overblown, from *Empire* magazine's William Thomas in 2004. "You want to know how far someone could go to wreak revenge? Well, we advise you to brave South Korean writer-director Park Chan-wook's helter-skelter descent into the dingiest pit of human behaviour, even if at times it is tough going and ludicrously unfeasible." The *Guardian*'s Peter Bradshaw, in a 5-star rave, was no less restrained, saying that the film "opens up a whole new sicko frontier of exotic horror, and more or less reduced my intestines to guacamole both times I watched it."

The reactions were extreme, and, indeed, *extreme* was the word of the day. On its release in the UK in 2004, *Oldboy* served as the high-water mark for a wave of theatrical and home video releases from distributor Tartan Films' imprint, Asia Extreme. Set up in the wake of the cult success of Hideo Nakata's J-horror gem *Ring* (1998), Asia Extreme sampled disparate genre offerings from across the region and gave it one, easily digestible umbrella term. More a masterstroke of marketing than a considered analysis of a filmmaking trend, it nevertheless influenced presumptions of Korean and Asian cinema among English-speaking audiences and critics. As Bradshaw writes, "*Oldboy* certainly shows that it's Asia where the farthest reaches of extreme cinema are to be found."

The endorsement of superfan Quentin Tarantino, who headed up the jury at 2004's Cannes Film Festival and awarded *Oldboy* the Grand Prix, no doubt contributed to the hype. Director Park Chan-wook, though, told *Sight and Sound* that the perceived tendency towards "hyperviolence" in Korean cinema was more "down to what Western distributors choose to show in the West". Looking at the Korean box office charts bears this out: in 2003, *Oldboy* was released alongside war films (*Silmido*), erotic dramas (*Untold Scandal*), dark thrillers (*Memories of Murder*) and rom-coms (*My Tutor Friend*).

However, in conversation with the Korean Film Council about his formative years, Park said: "It is not an exaggeration to say I was surrounded by violence." Born in Seoul in 1963 to a middle-class Catholic family, he was at high school and university during dark and troubling times in Korean history, from the Gwangju Uprising, where student demonstrations were violently quelled by military forces, to common stories of torture and self-immolation.

Park enrolled in the department of Philosophy at Sogang University, and developed an interest in photography and film. A viewing of Alfred Hitchcock's *Vertigo* (1958) at the university film club he founded was what made him want to make films himself. From then on, he was committed to

Above: Hammer time. Dae-su's weapon of choice has become a historic cinematic tool of vengeance.

Opposite, left and right bottom: Dae-su collapses after eating "a living thing"; Mi-do, who served up the wriggling delight, soon becomes a bigger part of Dae-su's life.

FURTHER VIEWING

The logical next step would be to dig deeper into Park Chan-wook's *Vengeance Trilogy* with *Sympathy for Mr. Vengeance* (2002) and *Lady Vengeance* (2005, pictured top right). Violent revenge thrillers are a staple of Korean cinema, with other gems including Kim Jee-woon's *A Bittersweet Life* (2005) and *I Saw the Devil* (2010), or the more action-packed *The Villainess* (2017), *The Man from Nowhere* (2010) and *The Gangster, the Cop, the Devil* (2019). Park Chan-wook has continued to be one of Korea's foremost filmmakers on the world cinema stage, but his career has taken some delightfully idiosyncratic turns, including a distinctive take on the vampire genre with *Thirst* (2009) and the odd, pastel-coloured romantic comedy-cum-psychodrama *I'm a Cyborg, But That's OK* (2006). Less divisive are his breakout blockbuster *Joint Security Area* (2000) and the erotic drama *The Handmaiden* (2016, pictured bottom right), adapted from the novel *Fingersmith* by Sarah Waters. Yet his recent film, the noirish romantic drama *Decision to Leave* (2022), with its bravura performances from leads Tang Wei and Park Hae-il, may come to be regarded as his masterpiece. It's certainly one of his most well-regarded: the film swept the Blue Dragon Awards and won three Grand Bell Awards, including Best Film, while Park himself picked up the Best Director prize at the Cannes Film Festival.

Above: Temple of doom. Woo-jin (Yoo Ji-tae), the film's central nefarious villain.

Opposite top: The hard cell. Before his entrapment, Dae-su worked as a businessman and had a family – a life that's gone.

cinema. Film critic Kim Young-jin first met him while they were at university, and in his book about Park he paints a distinctive picture: "Park is the proverbial 'guy who's seen too many movies,'" Kim writes. "He is one of those artists whose desire to watch movies is as strong as an appetite for food or sex." Kim characterizes Park as someone who prioritizes film above everything else, even his own projects, relating an anecdote that had Park rushing through a day's shooting schedule on *I'm A Cyborg, But That's OK* (2006), in order to clock off in time to catch a retrospective screening of Sam Peckinpah's *Straw Dogs* (1971) at a cinema on the other side of town.

After he graduated university, Park made his first inroads into the film industry, including working with Kwak Jae-yong as assistant director on *Watercolour Painting in a Rainy Day* (1989). Then, he laboured for five years at a production company in roles ranging from marketing and poster design to acquisitions and subtitling, under the assurance that they'd one day produce his debut film as director. That project was the gangster film *The Moon is... the Sun's Dream* (1992): a resounding flop. It took Park five years to secure backing for his second feature, during which time he had 10 scripts rejected by film companies, but even that film, 1997's *Trio*, was a failure.

Away from making films, Park had found success writing about them as a film critic. At his peak, he wrote columns for five of Korea's film magazines, and regularly appeared on the radio. During this time, he would become known as an authority on cult cinema, but his tastes were broad. He was just as likely to laud the work of Pedro Almodóvar as he was that of Sam Raimi or

Nicholas Ray, and his writing covered everything from *Alien 3* (1992) and *Attack of the Killer Tomatoes* (1978) to Jean-Luc Godard's *Contempt* (1963), and Kim Ki-young's underappreciated films, *Woman of Fire* (1971) and *Insect Woman* (1972).

But by the close of the decade, Park was prepared to trade it all in for one more shot at filmmaking, giving up the writing gigs and channelling all his efforts into his next project. As he told Kim Young-jin, "I was personally confronted with a major crisis . . . I needed to show that I could make a popular film, a well-made movie." That film was *Joint Security Area* (2000), a politically charged whodunnit thriller that drew inspiration from the tensions between North and South Korea. It was a resounding hit, breaking box office records with almost 6 million tickets sold, and eventually taking home the top prize at both the Blue Dragon and Grand Bell awards ceremonies. Once dismissed as a cult film geek, Park had finally broken through to the mainstream, and one of Korea's great auteurs was born.

REMAKES

As always happens when films and filmmakers from around the world garner attention and acclaim, Hollywood swoops in with its chequebook to buy up the remake rights. The 2013 English-language version of *Oldboy* (pictured), directed by the great American director Spike Lee, was a box office bomb that blunted the sharp edges of Park Chan-wook's original, while other Korean gems have been transformed into disposable Hollywood fodder, including *A Tale of Two Sisters* (*The Uninvited*), *Il Mare* (*The Lake House*), *Into the Mirror* (*Mirrors*) and *My Sassy Girl* (*My Sassy Girl*).

"I'm no punk, you know. How am I supposed to work a hairdo like that?!" That's what Choi Min-sik said to *Oldboy* hair department head Song Jong-hee when he saw the frazzled mop she had designed for him. And it's probably the most iconic hairstyle he'll ever have. Playing Oh Dae-su, a businessman with a wife and daughter, who gets imprisoned for 15 years for no apparent reason, Choi's zig-zagging mane (conceived as being previously a straight perm, now grown out to the extreme) is the perfect 'do for a character who seems to reverberate with rage, from deep inside all the way to his split ends.

Park Chan-wook's film is relentless and rewarding. Its hammer-blowing violence and gut-punching tragedy make for bruising viewing, but the way Park executes his executions is so skilful and at times beautiful, it's hard not to find all the mania alluring. Having watched the world through TV news for over a decade, practising his boxing against a brick wall and trying (and failing) to commit suicide, Dae-su is randomly released one day and like an alien – a feeling heightened by the bug-eyed sunglasses he steals – starts to tentatively, then ferociously, consume the new world of the 21st century.

Choi Min-sik's hyper-sensory performance is the fiercely beating heart of the film. Immediately searching for the identity of his abductors, he touches, smells and tastes his way through his investigation. One notorious scene, in which Dae-su wants to "eat a living thing", sees him chew through a real and wriggling octopus (as actor Choi actually did), served to him by Mi-do (Kang Hye-jung), a young chef. The scene is shot and performed with a matter-of-fact blankness, and we see a sense of power, and a stolen life, returning to Dae-su, who forms a bond with Mi-do, which gradually becomes romantic. Subordinate and indulging, Mi-do has a placidness that initially feels thinly sketched, but her characterization, and Dae-su's treatment of her, helps build to the film's sour denouement.

Although his protagonist commits violent acts, Park's direction of them is one of the film's biggest pleasures, not for their gore, but for their inventiveness. The fleshy fodder in Dae-su's escalating odyssey are a tool for toying with cinematic expectations of what viewers are, or are not, permitted to see. Dae-su takes out a team of henchmen in a hallway fight that remains the height of the genre (sorry, Vader), the camera gliding back and forth on a dolly in one shot, like a shadow play, with Choi its wheezing, buckling, but enduring hero. The faltering fighters and the unbroken flow makes this superpowered act feel real and lays a stylized, but realist, groundwork which means that when something close up and more extreme happens – say, for instance, someone cutting off their own tongue – the sight is off-screen but the pain is blinding. Playing further with filmic forecasting, in another attack the frame freezes and a red line, like a flight tracker in an *Indiana Jones* film, joins Dae-su's hammer (his weapon of choice, gripped with knuckles like dinner plates, flattened by all that time sparring with a wall) to his victim's head. The journey might be telegraphed, but the arrival lands outside the frame – with a stomach-churning crash.

To detail the narrative beats of *Oldboy* too much would be to destroy a lot of its tangled pleasure: Park's plotting is consistently surprising. That said, it's not necessarily the strongest element of the film, especially in its final act when rushed, late exposition and a convenient hypnotist are relied on to reach the finish line. For a more elegantly unfurled labyrinthine tale, seek out his 2016 film *The Handmaiden*, a tricksy, erotic drama with its own cephalopod pleasures, or 2022's more restrained, melancholy cat-and-mouse melodrama *Decision to Leave*. Compared to his earlier work, like in *Joint Security Area*, *Sympathy for Mr. Vengeance* and *Oldboy*, where compassion has cold, dire repercussions, Park's later films develop a warmer, romantic streak, although still not always a happy ending.

Dae-su is taunted with various ribboned boxes throughout the film, and unwrapping them eventually leads him to his answers and to his captor Woo-jin (Yoo Ji-tae). It is narratively, and literally, a "mystery box" film, the final punishing unboxing occurring at Woo-jin's brooding, sleek, Bond-villain penthouse – which even has its own interior moat. Celluloid cameras fill every bit of Woo-jin's shelf space, a reminder of a moment that kept his life in stasis, of traumatic memory and heartache, and something Dae-su had chosen to forget. Pain and memory are in every frame of this story, in the events that shape its characters, and in its style. It captures revenge in a way that is both passionate and disparate, with images clinging with clarity or entirely absent, like the photographs of an event and the memories of it.

Park's cult favourite is a landmark, for its impact in widening Western awareness of Korean cinema, for its berserker confidence inspiring action directors to punch higher, and for creating an icon for the ages in Dae-su and his hair ("My make-up team's contribution to the success of *Oldboy* was significant," says Song Jong-hee). Like those boxes that Dae-su receives, this is a film full of horrors, but it's packaged up incredibly. *Oldboy* is a gift.

Above: Choi Min-sik sporting the frizzy hair and hammer that have helped make Dae-su such an enduring creation.
Opposite: Park Chan-wook with the Grand Prix certificate awarded to him at the Cannes Film Festival in 2004.

A GIRL AT MY DOOR

....

도희야

UNLOCKING A MYSTERY

After being outed and accused of misconduct,
Lee Young-nam is transferred from Seoul to the
seaside town of Yeosu to take up the position of
local police chief. There, her life soon becomes
entangled with that of Do-hee, a young girl
who is being abused by her stepfather.

2014

Director: July Jung

119 mins

Ever since she was a young girl, July Jung wanted to be a film director. Born in 1980, she was a young member of the VHS generation, and vividly remembers her father renting films to watch one evening, which she would then watch herself the next day. These videos included the likes of Jane Campion's *The Piano* (1993), Jonathan Demme's *Philadelphia* (1993), and Chen Kaige's Chinese historical drama *Farewell My Concubine* (1993). "It was helpful that he didn't just watch one genre," she told Eastern Kicks. "He watched Hollywood films, European films, Korean films; in all genres. So I think that's when I realised that it would be something I'd want to do as well."

While studying at Seoul's Sungkyunkwan University, Jung would spend days at the Seoul Cinematheque, falling in love with the films of Pedro Almodóvar, Jean Renoir, Stanley Kubrick, David Lynch and Shōhei Imamura. Later, she enrolled in the Korea National University of Arts' film programme and studied under another one of her favourite filmmakers, Lee Chang-dong. There, she made a series of short films, including *A Man Under the Influenza* (2007), which won the Sonje award at the Busan International Film Festival. Towards the end of her studies, she had the chance to compete with other students to pitch a film project. She didn't win but received perhaps the best possible prize in the long run: Lee offered to produce her first feature at his production company, Pine House Film.

The feature, *A Girl at My Door*, was something of a homecoming for Jung, taking her back to her hometown of Yeosu on the south coast of Korea. The budget was low, and cobbled together from film councils and funding bodies, but the debut director had Lee as her mentor. "This film would not have been possible without his kind help, from casting to the completion," Jung told the Korean Film Council. "When I was in trouble, he would come to me quietly and comfort me by showing sympathy, and when it came to criticising, he would criticise me very specifically." One of those specific notes, she recalls, was to keep an eye on the film's final runtime: a significant point of feedback from a director whose own films have grown longer over the years (*Burning*, discussed later in this book, comes in at a zippy two-and-a-half hours).

Opposite: My policewoman. Almost as soon as Lee Young-nam arrives in Yeosu, her life becomes entangled with that of the troubled local girl, Do-hee.

Right, from top: Power trio. *A Girl at My Door* features three powerful performances from its central cast: Kim Sae-ron as Do-hee (top), Song Sae-byeok as her disreputable father (middle) and Bae Doona as the cop caught between them (bottom).

Another integral cornerstone of the film was lead actress Bae Doona (*Take Care of My Cat*, *The Host*), who read the script while shooting *Jupiter Ascending* with the Wachowskis in London. She loved what she read, and joined the project, waiving her usual movie-star fee. "I really wanted to be in this film and I wanted to see it at the cinema," she told Eye For Film. "I love working with first time directors. They collaborate with you a lot more and give you more to work with. Also, July is very strong – a quiet but strong woman. She's very calm but very sharp."

A Girl at My Door received its world premiere in the Un Certain Regard selection at the Cannes Film Festival in 2014, starting a global journey for a film that included stops at the Toronto and London Film Festivals. A UK release from LGBTQ+ specialist distributor Peccadillo Pictures later followed in 2015. In *Sight and Sound*, critic Tony Rayns wrote: "As a debut feature this is an achievement by any measure . . . Jung avoids clichés and platitudes. And then there's Bae Doona."

Above: Arresting drama. July Jung's complex portrayal of the relationship between Young-nam and Do-hee resists easy interpretation.

Opposite: Rising star. After working as a child actress in films such as *The Man From Nowhere*, Kim Sae-ron won acclaim for her performance as the inscrutable young girl, Do-hee.

FURTHER VIEWING ⬤

July Jung (pictured) and Bae Doona reunited in 2022 for the drama *Next Sohee*, another film that intertwines the stories of a young woman and an older police investigator, but this time inspired by the real-life tragedy of a high-school student driven to suicide by a toxic workplace environment. While the fight for LGBT rights in Korea continues, the field of films addressing themes and characters from these backgrounds is growing, from the high-school horror of *Memento Mori* (1999) to the groundbreaking *No Regret* (2006), which was the first Korean feature directed by an openly gay filmmaker, and from the erotic thriller *The Handmaiden* (2016) to the low-key dramas *Our Love Story* (2016), *House of Hummingbird* (2018) and *Moonlit Winter* (2019).

A GIRL AT MY DOOR – REVIEW

Police chief Lee Young-nam (Bae Doona) has moved from Seoul to a small fishing village, and when she makes one of her first arrests there, it's not a glamorous movie-cop moment. It's an awkward, late night gangling mess of confused shouting bodies – realist and wriggling. Fascinating, sinister and enduringly debatable, *A Girl at My Door* is like that arrest: dark and very hard to wrestle with.

Scanning every room she goes into with suspicion, Chief Lee is a mysterious figure, arriving in town under veiled circumstances, staying sober and silent at karaoke, instead preferring the solitude of home and giant water bottles full of decanted soju. When Sun Do-hee (Kim Sae-ron), a local girl and victim of domestic abuse, comes to her for help, Lee welcomes her into her home, despite the fact that Sun's adopted father seems to have some unspoken, underworld stranglehold on the wellbeing of the village. Ominously told by her superior officers to "watch [herself] in shallower waters", Lee's initial act of kindness warps into a tangle of maternal and professional navigation, impropriety and sociopolitical destruction.

The chief starts living with Sun, seeing in her perhaps both a daughter and mirror. They get the same haircut, they share baths, they even have their own nocturnal vices – dancing and performance for Sun, alcohol for Lee – to help them get through their pained nights. The allure of this haven, and of this companionship, is shot in a grounded, unfussy and intimate manner, with Lee's isolated, harshly lit drinking sessions providing a noirish contrast. That darker, uneasy aspect of the film creeps up, and takes over its second half as revelations about Lee's homosexuality, the exploitation of illegal immigrants by Sun's father, and the ripples caused by big political actions in a small town, lead to the chief herself getting arrested.

Reframed in a superbly cross-cut pair of interrogation scenes, Lee and Sun's relationship is given a different reading – not of generosity, but rather the calmly exploited appropriation of parenthood, with Lee's sexuality read as a potential threat to the phobic town. From there, the moral thorniness gets even more barbed, with Bae Doona magnificently pivoting between fear, pride and love towards Sun as alarming acts of revenge, hidden truths and compromised, supposed justice form a gripping finale. As a car drives off towards the horizon, with a surprising amount of destruction in its wake, a single, superb look asks who's being protected – those in the car, or those being left? Fantastically fearless, July Jung's film is must-watch, and morally murky viewing.

RIGHT NOW, WRONG THEN

지금은맞고그때는틀리다

TWO FOR ONE

A film director, Chun-su, travels to Suwon to deliver a lecture and screen his work at a film festival. However, he arrives a day early, and instead he meets a young artist, Hee-jung, and they spend the day together. The same day is played out twice, with different dramatic outcomes.

2015

Director: Hong Sang-soo

112 mins

There are many Korean filmmakers famed for their prolific output. Across their long careers, Shin Sang-ok and Im Kwon-taek amassed over 70 and 100 director credits, respectively. In recent decades, though, there is one director that stands out: Hong Sang-soo, who since his debut in 1996 has polished off the equivalent of at least one film a year. As of 2022, he has released 28 features, and is showing little sign of slowing down.

If that makes you feel unaccomplished, take heart from the fact that Hong was a late bloomer. His debut film, 1996's *The Day a Pig Fell into a Well*, was released when he was 35, and his route to directing was wayward, if not entirely unexpected.

Hong was born in Seoul in 1960, and later in that decade his parents ran a production company, producing 76 films between 1964 and 1969, including Lee Man-hee's *A Day Off*. Hong's parents divorced when he was young, and he was brought up by his mother and maternal grandmother. After a directionless youth marked by depression, young Hong initially failed his college entrance exams, before studying at Chung-Ang University in Seoul – majoring first in theatre, then switching to film.

He then moved to the United States, studying at the California College of the Arts (CCA) and then as a graduate at the School of the Art Institute of Chicago (SAIC). It was at the latter institution that he discovered the work of French post-impressionist painter Paul Cézanne, whose work would prove to be a lifelong inspiration. It was also during these years that Hong was moved by the work of filmmakers such as Robert Bresson, Yasujirō Ozu, Carl Theodor Dreyer and Éric Rohmer, and writers ranging from Anton Chekhov and Fyodor Dostoevsky to Ernest Hemingway and Albert Camus.

Once he moved back to Korea in the 1990s, he started working for his mother's production company producing work for television, before committing himself to film and making his debut with *The Day the Pig Fell into the Well* (a debut, too, of sorts, for Song Kang-ho, who appears in a small role). While not a box office hit, the film was well received: Hong won the Best New Director prize at that year's Blue Dragon Film Awards (shared with Kang Je-gyu for *Gingko Bed*), and the film magazine *Cine21* likened the film's release to "a gunshot that shook Korean film history". Hong found himself at the forefront of a new generation of Korean filmmakers. He also quickly became one of the more visible arthouse directors on the international stage, picking up the prestigious Tiger Award at the Rotterdam International Film Festival, alongside screenings in Vancouver, Tokyo and Berlin.

In contrast to his contemporaries who have enjoyed commercial or cult success, Hong's renown has been built and sustained on the international festival trail. His second film, *The Power of Hangwon Province*, won Best Director and Best Screenplay at the Blue Dragon Film Awards, but it was also his first film to screen at the Cannes Film Festival, setting in motion a drift towards international acclaim over domestic success. His films have since won prizes at Cannes (*Hahaha*) and major film festivals in Berlin (*The Woman Who Ran, Introduction, The Novelist's Film*), San Sebastian (*Yourself and Yours*) and Locarno (*Right Now, Wrong Then*), and through the 2010s and beyond it has become almost a given that a new Hong Sang-soo film, or two, will premiere across a year's festival calendar.

Hong's distinctive filmmaking style and prolific work rate found their form once he established his own production company, Jeonwonsa, which launched with the 2005 feature *Tale of Cinema*. While not impenetrable, his films were never destined to be blockbusters: they're low budget, quickly made, simply shot, unassuming, yet discreetly experimental, and they often return to familiar themes in new framings, with no grand pronouncements made or lessons given. "The best thing for a film to tell us is that life cannot be explained," Hong once told the Korean Film Council, and he elaborated to critic Huh Moon-young that his films are "not made to express a story, but to feature some fragments. I take those so-called fragments and with them derive a whole structure centred on everyday situations."

Over the years, Hong stopped writing full screenplays for his films, slowly transitioning towards a practice that revolved around spontaneity. Production starts with treatments, outlines, sometimes just titles or, as Dennis Lim describes in his study of *Tale of Cinema* "an inciting spark, which can be a narrative or formal element or a vague sensation". The director often leaves writing scripts for scenes until the morning of the shoot, a decision that he self-deprecatingly told Huh Moon-young came from laziness more than anything: "I think I was lazy my whole life. I would procrastinate as much as I can. At the last moment, when I can no longer procrastinate, some spontaneous thing happens in my actions. I always liked that."

He may call it laziness, but even so, it is in keeping with Hong's signature style: organic and yet wholly his own. It's no accident that, as years and films have gone by, his credits have expanded as the apparatus of filmmaking has been stripped away. Today, it's not uncommon for him to supplement his roles as director and writer with those of producer, cinematographer, editor and even soundtrack composer. The French actress Isabelle Huppert, who has worked with Hong twice (on *In Another Country* and *Claire's Camera*), perhaps puts it best in her testimonial for Dennis

Lim's book, *Tale of Cinema*: "With Hong Sang-soo less is more. Less time to shoot, fewer explanations, fewer people on set – more inspiration, more cinema... with Hong, it is about getting to what's essential. Poetry, humour, emotion."

Opposite: Kim Min-hee and Jung Jae-young lead this edition of Hong's recurring roster of actors.

Above: Kim Min-hee, alongside Hong Sang-soo. Kim won the Silver Bear award at the 2017 Berlin Film Festival for her role in Hong's film *On the Beach at Night Alone*.

FURTHER VIEWING

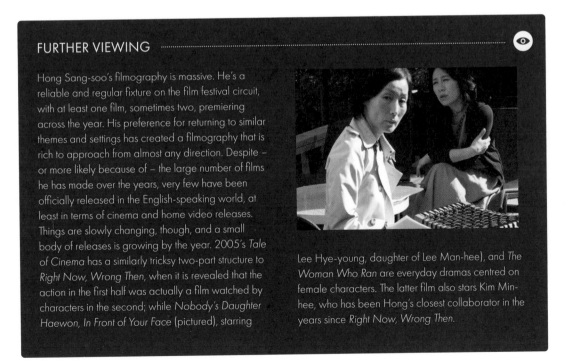

Hong Sang-soo's filmography is massive. He's a reliable and regular fixture on the film festival circuit, with at least one film, sometimes two, premiering across the year. His preference for returning to similar themes and settings has created a filmography that is rich to approach from almost any direction. Despite – or more likely because of – the large number of films he has made over the years, very few have been officially released in the English-speaking world, at least in terms of cinema and home video releases. Things are slowly changing, though, and a small body of releases is growing by the year. 2005's *Tale of Cinema* has a similarly tricksy two-part structure to *Right Now, Wrong Then*, when it is revealed that the action in the first half was actually a film watched by characters in the second; while *Nobody's Daughter Haewon*, *In Front of Your Face* (pictured), starring

Lee Hye-young, daughter of Lee Man-hee), and *The Woman Who Ran* are everyday dramas centred on female characters. The latter film also stars Kim Min-hee, who has been Hong's closest collaborator in the years since *Right Now, Wrong Then*.

When I watch a Hong Sang-soo film, I feel like I'm going back to my hometown. I feel comfortable, awaiting both the satisfaction of the recognizable, and anticipating the new. I'll see familiar faces, walk familiar streets and drink (maybe a few too many) familiar drinks. But each time I go back something has changed. Those people I recognize from before have a different job now, with new vices and goals, but the same foundational traits; the coffee shops and bars feel the same, but with a different coat of paint; and anyone new who arrives seem to fit in with the crowd straight away.

In mainstream cinema the concept of a shared cinematic universe has swallowed up the blockbuster. Caught between franchise entries, the likes of Marvel or DC reap and sow narratives for films past and future, occasionally finding time to tell a story in between, with a litany of characters from their back catalogue ready to pop up at the drop of a contractual obligation. The Hong cinematic universe, however, is a far more curious realm. It's a place where people, locations and actions will seemingly repeat, albeit with slight variations, in a number of different films – sometimes within the same film. Realities can collapse, time can be resculpted and stories can be replayed again and again, all without

any of the temporal juggling smugness of a Christopher Nolan film. In *Tale of Cinema*, the first half of the film is revealed to be a film within a film, and the second half sees characters echo the events of the fiction that preceded them. In *On the Occasion of Remembering the Turning Gate* a character is told a local legend, and the back half of the story sees them retrace it. Hong's films often come with a Side A and a Side B, films that are divided in the middle, with stories ready to be flipped.

Hong's 2015 film *Right Now, Wrong Then* is a great entry to the Hong Universe and it joins this bifurcated collection, split down the middle, with similar events, occurring to the same characters, being told and then retold in a game of cinephilic spot the difference. The film's first half is preceded with the title *Right Then, Wrong Now*, the second half gets the title *Right Now, Wrong Then*. From its beginning comes one of many compounding intrigues that make this one of Hong's most compelling, revisitable works. Ham Cheon-soo, played with a deftly revealed sliminess by Jung Jae-young, is a filmmaker (a common profession for Hong's characters) who spends the day with painter Yoon Hee-jung (Kim Min-hee), his seemingly poetic pursuance leading to an embarrassing downfall. The second hour of the film sees this day play out again, with slight changes in behaviour, reshaping the events.

The characters and settings remain the same, but the playthrough is different, as if we're having another go at a lecherous RPG. What is the nature of these worlds? Are they nested? Parallel? Memory? Fiction?

Hong isn't worried about the physics, or the how, of these two realms, just what they can show us. In the first half, a character says, "There's no such thing as important words," but the film shows the opposite: the butterfly effect of communication. In one reality alcohol, infidelity and even the treatment of a post-film Q&A are navigated a certain way, but thanks to seemingly minor changes in dialogue, that path is very different when played through again. There's both originality and fatefulness to the second path, like many Hong films before it. Here, a man's drunkenness, overfamiliarity, deception ("you strike me as a very honest man," winks one character) and abrupt confessions blow up in his face, and even with the story replayed, he still exposes himself (quite literally).

Both Jung Jae-young and Kim Min-hee are excellent, and during simply framed, static extended takes, their rapport lures and ensconces viewers in Hong's world. While cocksure and sly in part one, Cheon-soo is a more brash and unpredictable figure in part two, Jung's observant performance feeling like factions of the same man, built on the same insecurities, rather than two separate ones. Kim Min-hee's performance sees its own shift; from quite forthright and innocent, she pivots into a

more subdued and melancholy mode – perhaps the déjà vu has kicked in?

Visually, *Right Now, Wrong Then* features some Hong staple cinematographic techniques that, despite their common usage, maintain their weight. A zoom at the start of the film projects Cheon-soo's leering gaze, while a later, almost comic use, at a moment of disappointing revelation, punches with disappointment and regret. A typical Hong image of two bodies, sat at a table, framed by the blown-out light of a window recurs, the everyday, yet dramatic framing enriching the microdramas of the dialogue. Hong has said he tries not to make things "too beautiful", but he can't help find elegance in his mundanity. One shot in particular, of Hee-jung slumped in the glow of a table lamp after too much to drink, reveals isolation in a glowing, dreamy warmth.

It is – unfortunately for Hong – a beautifully composed image, one we luckily get to witness twice, and perhaps one that will be seen again and again, as this beguiling cinematic universe continues to expand, return and enrich with each entry, new and old.

Opposite: Two characters, deep in conversation, held in an extended take. A fixture of Hong's filmography.

Above: Infinite worlds possible. Retelling, remixing, reliving. Like many of Hong's films, *Right Now, Wrong Then* features a story being retold.

VETERAN

베테랑

POLICE STORY

A tenacious cop sets his sights on taking down an arrogant, affluent heir to a major corporation who is involved in dodgy dealings behind the scenes.

2015
Director: Ryoo Seung-wan
123 mins

When film critic Kim Young-jin asked Park Chan-wook about *Oldboy*'s now-legendary single-take corridor fight scene, the director described action sequences as "a pain", vowing never to attempt such a thing again: "How can I hope to match Ryoo Seung-wan in the direction of dazzling and complicated action setpieces?"

Once dubbed Korean cinema's "action kid", Ryoo Seung-wan (pictured below) stands apart from many of his fellow film-nuts-turned-directors thanks to his lifelong love of action cinema, something kick-started at a young age when he saw the films of Bruce Lee, Jackie Chan and the Shaw Brothers. Born in 1973, young Ryoo saw Chan's breakout hit *Drunken Master* (1978) while he was still in primary school, and was immediately inspired to study martial arts himself, training in taekwondo. Later, he bought an 8mm camera and made amateur films starring himself and his younger brother, actor Ryoo Seung-bum. He continued to watch films voraciously, everything from Buster Keaton's *Our Hospitality* (1923) to Sergio Leone's *Once Upon a Time in the West* (1968) to Shōhei Imamura's *Vengeance is Mine* (1979).

After his parents passed away, he dropped out of high school to support his family, performing odd jobs before slowly moving closer to the film industry. Park Chan-wook, then more successful as a film critic than a filmmaker, took him under his wing, and Ryoo worked on Bong Joon-ho's short film *Incoherence* (1994), Park's second feature *Trio* (1997) and Park Ki-hyung's

Whispering Corridors (1998), all the while cutting his teeth on shorts such as *Transmutated Head* (shot by Jang Joon-hwan, then a film student) and the series of films that would be recut into his breakthrough debut feature, *Die Bad* (2000).

In his films, Ryoo aimed to combine the technique of John Woo, the stunts of Jackie Chan, the cinematic rhythms of Martin Scorsese and the stylish storytelling of Quentin Tarantino, all shot through with the budget-conscious economy of Roger Corman and Robert Rodriguez. Following *Die Bad*, Ryoo worked consistently, eventually setting up the production company Filmmaker R&K with his co-producer and wife, Kang Hye-jung. In 2008, he told the Korean Film Council: "A director is a person who works with the heart of an artist, the brain of a capitalist, and the hands and feet of a labourer".

Ryoo's ninth film, 2015's *Veteran*, broke through to an unprecedented degree. Envisioned as a tribute to the heroic action flicks of his youth, *Veteran* sold over 13 million tickets on release, the most of any film, Korean or otherwise, that year, and it shot into the Top 5 of the highest-grossing films of all time at the Korean box office. Today, Ryoo doesn't shy away from the "action kid" nickname, but he prefers to broaden the term a bit, telling Hangul Celluloid on the eve of *Veteran*'s UK premiere at the London East Asia Film Festival, "Action is a way of creating an emotion through moving pictures. For me, action isn't just a genre, it's so much more."

FURTHER VIEWING

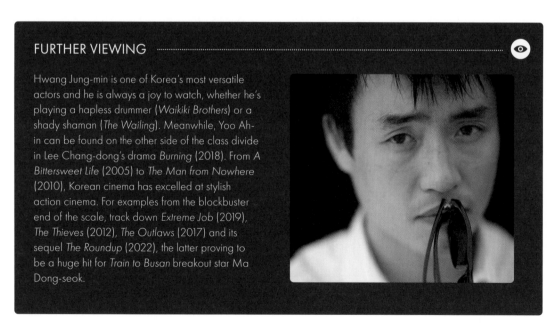

Hwang Jung-min is one of Korea's most versatile actors and he is always a joy to watch, whether he's playing a hapless drummer (*Waikiki Brothers*) or a shady shaman (*The Wailing*). Meanwhile, Yoo Ah-in can be found on the other side of the class divide in Lee Chang-dong's drama *Burning* (2018). From *A Bittersweet Life* (2005) to *The Man from Nowhere* (2010), Korean cinema has excelled at stylish action cinema. For examples from the blockbuster end of the scale, track down *Extreme Job* (2019), *The Thieves* (2012), *The Outlaws* (2017) and its sequel *The Roundup* (2022), the latter proving to be a huge hit for *Train to Busan* breakout star Ma Dong-seok.

Above: Criminal ties. Taking the corporate world to task, the judicial limit in *Veteran* reaches to the wealthy inhabitants of the tallest sky-scrapers.

Below: Out of office. Seo Do-cheol (Hwang Jung-min) takes to one of the many streets he's aiming to clear up.

VETERAN – REVIEW

Stylish, hilarious and politically engaged, *Veteran* is a crowd-pleasing police drama that slyly evolves from slapstick farce into gripping procedural commentary. Taking hold instantly with an opening involving espionage, car chases, the spectacularly violent use of a mechanic's tools and the slinky bass and rolling organ of a heist film, *Veteran* kicks off in flashy and jovial style. Following a team of cops led by the relentless but chipper Seo Do-cheol (Hwang Jung-min, brilliant in both *Waikiki Brothers* and *The Wailing*, too), the squad deal out justice, sassy quips and the occasional, perfectly timed pratfall. However, when investigating a lorry driver's apparent attempted suicide, the case entwines Seo with the ultra-rich, violent, spoiled heir to a conglomerate (Jo Tae-oh, played by Yoo Ah-in, unrecognizable from his standout role in *Burning*), who may have thrown the driver punches instead of the money his company owed him.

With cameos from a life-size statue of Heath Ledger as the Joker, as well as a model replica of the iconic, tank-like Tumbler, the film's earlier scenes nod to the dark shadow of Christopher Nolan's *Batman* films. Why so serious? Considering its first act feels more like an episode of comedy cop favourite *Brooklyn Nine-Nine*, Ledger's hunched figure comes as a surprise, but it sets up the film's evolving ambition, migrating into a starker, grimier thriller for its second half. Moving from comically stylized form, including a scene transition that looks like a page turning, the cinematography adopts a cooler, moodier approach as Seo's work travels from the streets to the sky-scraping executives. As the investigation deepens, his jokiness dissipates while Jo's bullying spirals, becoming more violent and erratic. Breaking ankles, humiliating women and speaking in LinkedIn proverbs, Yoo Ah-in offers a slimy, maniacal and paternally grovelling performance that could be right at home in *Succession*.

It's not perfect, the conspiracy does get a bit tangled, and the single female police officer gets tasked with doling out flying kicks and exposition, but it's always very entertaining – especially the final showdown featuring a brief appearance from *Train to Busan*'s Ma

Dong-seok. Presenting us with workers taking on the super-wealthy (not, you know, a multimillionaire loner in a cowl) while fighting for the life and honour of a union member labourer, *Veteran*'s seemingly small stakes but high intensity and passion is invigorating. A moral fight, framed like a world-ending event, puts superhero perils and style within a grounded plot of the wealthy exploiting the working class, which is unfortunately very believable, and still hugely entertaining.

Opposite: Yoo Ah-in (right) plays Jo Tae-oh, a slick and confident business overlord, very different to his role in *Burning*.

Above: Beyond *Veteran*, discover more of Hwang Jung-min's impressive range by watching *Waikiki Brothers* and *The Wailing*.

THE TRUTH BENEATH

비밀은 없다

BURIED SECRETS

Kim Yeon-hong is married to an aspiring politician who is running for office. When their daughter mysteriously goes missing mere weeks before the elections, Yeon-hong decides to take matters into her own hands.

2016

Director: Lee Kyoung-mi

102 mins

유력한 후보
사라진 딸,
15일 간의 미스터리

비밀은 없다

2016.06.23

손예진 / 김주혁   제작 영화사 게이 외유로제이판   제공·배급 C.J엔터테인먼트   〈미쓰 홍당무〉 이경미 감독

Some of the filmmakers discussed in this book dreamed of becoming directors from a young age; others came to it later in life. But few would describe their entry into filmmaking as an accident. Yet that's how Lee Kyoung-mi tells it: a friend was considering applying for film school, so she thought she'd try it out, too. "I followed her out of curiosity," she told HanCinema, "and managed to pass the entrance examination."

As a kid, Lee had never considered a career in film. Instead she longed to go into theatre as an actor, but her father, a theatre director, forbade her from pursuing the arts – leading to her studying Russian at the Hankuk University of Foreign Studies. Her love of film had been ignited by Luc Besson's French drama *The Big Blue* (1988), which she recalls renting from a video store and watching five times in quick succession, and she counts among her favourite filmmakers Claude Chabrol, the Coen brothers and Woody Allen. However, the prospect of studying film at the Korea National University of Arts, she remembered in an interview with *Cine21*, offered her an opportunity: perhaps she could start with film, and move to a theatre school afterwards.

Whatever her plans were to start with, though, she stuck with filmmaking. Between 2000 and 2003, she directed five short films, culminating in *Feel Good Story*, which won prizes at the Seoul International Women's Film Festival and the Mise-en-scène Short Film Festival. It was at the latter festival that Lee met director Park Chan-wook, who would become a key mentor as she moved into feature filmmaking. Lee worked with Park as a script supervisor and assistant director on *Lady Vengeance* (2005), the third film in his *Vengeance Trilogy*, and Park produced Lee's feature debut, *Crush and Blush* (2008; its Korean title is *Miss Hongdangmu*, literally "Miss Carrot").

Crush and Blush premiered at the Busan International Film Festival, and later won Best New Director and Best Screenplay at the Blue Dragon Film Awards. Attracting over half a million viewers on release, it was more of a cult hit than a blockbuster, but it has its fans, not least its producer. When asked in 2022 to recommend a "hidden gem" for *Sight and Sound* magazine's Korean Cinema special issue, Park Chan-wook wrote: "I always mention this film when someone outside South Korea asks me for a film recommendation. It's unique on every level... And as a comedy, there has never been a funnier film in South Korean cinema, period."

Lee and Park's collaboration continued with her 2016 feature, the more commercially minded thriller *The Truth Beneath*, where Park has a co-writer credit, although reportedly his most important contribution was the inciting logline for the project: a missing-person case in the middle of an election campaign. Park's patronage and that intriguing

pitch attracted investors, and allowed Lee to follow her own vision. "I began the story with the mother who lost her child," she told Narjas Zatat of the *Independent* as the film screened at the London Korean Film Festival. "I thought about the emotions that one event would produce: it would be devastating, horrifying and painful for the mother who lost her child. She would turn mad. I wanted to convey these emotions within the context of South Korean societal problems, while at the same time making it more personal... It is a story of the last hope in an otherwise cruel and devastating world."

Above: When his daughter disappears, a conspiracy balloons around politician Kim Jong-chan.

Opposite: Co-written by Park Chan-wook, Lee Kyoung-mi's film is labyrinthine, stylish and very satisfying.

FURTHER VIEWING ⊙

As a filmmaker, Lee Kyoung-mi (pictured) is something of a moving target. The feature film she made before *The Truth Beneath*, 2008's *Crush and Blush*, is an idiosyncratic workplace comedy about a high-school teacher unlucky in love (and often prone to being very red-faced), and in the years since she has left features behind for projects with Netflix, including the quirky fantasy series *The School Nurse Files*. So for more of the dark twists and turns of *The Truth Beneath*, it's best to look to the director's mentor, Park Chan-wook, and his 2022 neo-noir *Decision to Leave*, or to another film that trades in buried secrets, *Memories of Murder* (2003), from director Bong Joon-ho (who, it so happens, has a cameo in *Crush and Blush*).

THE TRUTH BENEATH – REVIEW

The web of conspiracy in a political thriller is normally one that spins outwards. A break-in results in a resignation. A hacker uncovers a matrix of deceit. A parking cop, who happens to be an animated rabbit, reveals institutional, xenophobic policy. In *The Truth Beneath*, the web contracts: what appears as a standard political thriller becomes something far more intimate and raw, with a brutal and tragic personal drama at its centre.

When a charismatic aspiring politician's daughter goes missing, his wife Kim Yeon-hong (Son Ye-jin) bears the brunt of the investigation, while her husband Kim Jong-chan (Kim Joo-hyuk) continues his campaign trail, contributing little to either the case or his family's grief, seeking out photo ops instead. Lee Kyoung-mi's story, co-written with Park Chan-wook, spends its first half in the stylish, comfortable realm of the police procedural, before a pile of rugs are individually pulled out over its second hour, in a dizzying conspiracy that burrows into Yeon-hong's loss.

The film is gripping throughout, and in terms of style, the directorial fingerprints of Lee's mentor are all over this mystery. Viewers familiar with Park Chan-wook's penchant for divided screens, elaborate scene transitions and on-screen graphics (in this case the fantastically deployed waveform of a lie detector) will recognize the director's influence, but Lee uses these tools for her own distinct tale. A consistent return to one point perspective keeps viewers centrally focused on forensic details, or glaring eyes bouncing straight back down the lens. This rigid composure reflects Yeon-hong's own, and when her world and beliefs start to contort, so, too, does Lee's visual language. Scenes rewind, day turns to night in seconds, and images and memories start to overlap, blend and blur, before truth comes into focus. Utilizing distinct props, costumes and make-up to powerful effect, the film's mise-en-scène subtly carries narrative weight through the turmoil. The bright pink of a headphone cable moves from utility item to a jewel of cross-generational emotion; differently deployed red make-up transforms Yeon-hong from pain to power; and clashing nylon jackets distinguish rival political parties, dressed like sports teams, highlighting the juvenile and tribalistic sporting culture that elections create.

Unpredictable and entirely engrossing, it's an excellent and angry political drama, but with so much beneath. There's a surprising emotional purity and poignant melodramatic tragedy, hidden under the chilling mystery (an avenue Park Chan-wook would further explore in 2022's *Decision to Leave*), which gives the film more heart and more weight than a standard conspiracy thriller. Told in a refreshing manner, Lee's film uses the depths of personal tragedy to underscore the darkness of election tactics, and the victims caught in the shrapnel of political hubris.

THE WAILING

곡성

CACOPHONY FOR THE DEVIL

Officer Jong-goo investigates a series
of grisly murders in the small village of
Gokseong, which might have been caused
by the influence of an evil demon.

2016

Director: Na Hong-jin

156 mins

A FILM BY NA HONG JIN

哭聲
곡성
THE WAILING

KWAK DO WON   HWANG JUNG MIN   KUNIMURA JUN   CHUN WOO HEE

"There's nothing scarier than not knowing what you should be scared of," wrote critic Maggie Lee for *Variety* when *The Wailing* premiered at the Cannes Film Festival in 2016, a week after its chart-topping release in Korea. The other Korean films in the Cannes selection that year, the zombie horror *Train to Busan* and Park Chan-wook's psychological drama *The Handmaiden*, offered distinctive spins on familiar genres – but *The Wailing* was something else. Part police procedural, part occult horror, the film was a beguiling and harrowing discovery that left audiences rattled and full of questions.

Director Na Hong-jin was hardly an unknown quantity, though. Born in Seoul in 1974, young Hong-jin dreamed of becoming a comics artist, and eventually worked in the advertising industry, until the day he quit his day job and committed himself to pursuing a career in filmmaking. He started writing screenplays, enrolled in the Korea National University of Arts, and made the short films *5 Minutes* (2003), *A Perfect Red Snapper Dish* (2005) and *Sweat* (2007), which won acclaim and netted prizes at the Grand Bell Awards and the Mise-en-scène Short Film Festival.

His feature debut, the serial-killer thriller *The Chaser* (2008), topped the Korean box office and ended the year the third highest-grossing domestic release. It swept the Grand Bell Awards, picking up five prizes including Best Film, Director and Actor, and screened at Cannes, attracting a few international fans along the way, including film critic Roger Ebert and director Christopher Nolan. Na had drawn inspiration from the gritty crime thrillers of filmmakers Takeshi Kitano, Kinji Fukasaku and William Friedkin, and now found himself touted as the genre's rising star.

His follow-up, the violent drama *The Yellow Sea* (2010), was a strained production marked by the director's perfectionist tendencies. Post-production had to be rushed in order to meet the film's release date – and yet the director still tinkered away on his edit, releasing a director's cut later in the year. On release, *The Yellow Sea* was received warmly by some critics, but back home it divided audiences. A planned transfer to Hollywood to helm a film for 20th Century Fox (which online speculation suggests was a sequel in the Liam Neeson *Taken* franchise) was put on hold while the director went back to the drawing board.

For such a wild, confounding horror film, *The Wailing* has deeply personal roots. Following the release of *The Yellow Sea*, Na Hong-jin suffered several bereavements in quick succession, which put him in a reflective, soul-searching mood. He had been brought up Christian but developed an interest in Asian folk religions, especially their relationships with death and the afterlife. He explained to *The Playlist*: "The questions raised during those days coincided with the things I have always been wondering while making my previous films. The question was, 'Why did THEY have to be victims OF ALL PEOPLE'? I already had the answers for the 'How'. What I had to find out was the 'Why'."

His thoughts drifted back to his childhood, when he would visit his grandmother's hometown of Gokseong, a small village in the mountains with a strong Catholic community. "It was very important to me where the film took place," he told Screen Daily. "It talks about the supernatural, of feeling it around you, and the truth. Gokseong is a place where you can get a feeling of religion and the supernatural. I thought it would be a good place to talk about Korean ghosts and gods, showing the changes in time and weather."

The result was far from a standard genre film. As he did in both his previous features, Na Hong-jin bent convention to his creative purpose. In conversation with Screen Daily on the occasion of *The Wailing*'s Cannes premiere, he acknowledged the influence of several significant occult horror films from Hollywood – *The Exorcist* (1973), *The Shining* (1980), *The Omen* (1976) and *Rosemary's Baby* (1968) – referring to them as "like textbooks". But his intent was clear: to put a Korean "twist on the canon".

FURTHER VIEWING

Perfectly poised as it is between two often overlapping genres, *The Wailing* presents something of a fork in the road. You can either venture down the path of the dark thriller, with Bong Joon-ho's *Memories of Murder* and Park Chan-wook's *Vengeance Trilogy* (*Sympathy for Mr. Vengeance*, *Oldboy*, *Lady Vengeance*), or you can plumb the depths of Korean supernatural horror with the likes of *Whispering Corridors*, *Into the Mirror*, *Phone* and *Suddenly in the Dark*, the latter of which also introduces heady doses of shamanic strangeness into the proceedings. Na Hong-jin's (pictured) debut film, *The Chaser*, is just as relentless and suspenseful as *The Wailing*, but offers more grounded, street-level thrills, setting pulses racing with breathless action, bone-crunching violence and frenetic editing.

Above: Horror comes home. When Jong-goo's daughter becomes possessed, the supernatural threat becomes all too real.

Below: Stormy weather. *The Wailing* immerses the viewer in the weather and landscape of its regional setting.

Above: Stranger by the Lake. Jun Kunimura stars
as the mysterious, unnamed Japanese man.

THE WAILING – REVIEW

During a forest police chase, as a potential perpetrator sits tantalizingly close and cloying thick woodland dials up the tension, out of nowhere one of the team is struck by lightning. A sign from God, maybe? One thing it undoubtedly telegraphs is that in *The Wailing*, anything can happen.

In the remote mountain village of Gokseong, coinciding with the new residency of a Japanese man (Jun Kunimura), a mysterious infection starts to take hold of people, transforming them into bulbous, murderous, demons who take the lives of their families in gruesome style. Jong-goo (Kwak Do-won) is the police officer in charge of the case, one that's far bigger and far grislier than anything that normally bothers his modest patrol. Initially having the colder, absorbingly murky procedural manner of Bong Joon-ho's *Memories of Murder* (about Korea's first serial murder case) by way of *Fargo's* quaint darkness, the nature of the case soon mutates.

Becoming convinced that something more than an infection is causing the crimewave, Jong-goo enlists the help of Japanese-speaking deacon Yang I-sam (Kim Do-yoon), to help investigate the Japanese man's house. In a gruellingly tense sequence, accompanied by a relentless barking dog, they discover a wall of victim photographs, their belongings and a sacrificial chamber; a brutal interrogation, a canine murder and a moral line crossing soon follow. Jong-goo's daughter's shoe is discovered as one of the ritualistic items and she becomes infected, or perhaps possessed, and the film becomes a race against time, and across genres, in an attempt to find a cure.

Elegantly wandering through murder mystery, faith drama, ghost story, zombie flick and social commentary, *The Wailing* has a scope that is enormous, but its 156 minutes never feel bloated. It's a patient, exhilarating work, which maintains its own unique steadily consuming atmosphere while bouncing in so many story directions. Legendary cinematographer Hong Kyung-pyo (whose remarkable résumé also includes Lee Chang-Dong's *Burning*, Bong Joon-ho's *Parasite* and Hirokazu Kore-eda's *Broker*) lures viewers in with eerie wides, absorbing in urban and natural detail but which also camouflage minute terrors upon closer inspection. Editor Kim Sun-min (who assembled *Memories of Murder*) must be celebrated as well because some of the most memorable sequences are created by their exemplary work. Standout sequences involving shaman rituals are reminiscent of the heady cross-cutting anxiety created by the now iconic sacrifice montage of *Apocalypse Now* as the film ascends from simmering paranoia to a furious boil of drumming, dancing, and a whole lot of wailing. As dread and vengeance seep through the village, the fingers point in all directions – at the shaman himself, a mysterious white-clad woman, some nearby deadly mushrooms and the Japanese man. Blame shifts between curses, Christian devils and nature itself, but the cause of *The Wailing* is less important than the infection – fear and hate, the xenophobic response to the outsider (never given a name, always just "Japanese man") beginning the spiral into mania.

Considering its length and depth, *The Wailing* might also seem like a thing to be afraid of, but among the madness is a lot of fun as well. Kwak Do-won shows his skill as a comedic actor, his police officer's foibles and fears grounding the film's first act in bumbling authenticity, and in turn making his descent into violent madness all the more shocking. And later, one sequence, in which a reanimated corpse attacks Jong-goo and friends – featuring buckets of blood and a gnarly use of a garden rake – adds to the menagerie of threats piling onto Gokseong, but will also cheerily satisfy any George Romero fans in search of some good old-fashioned zombie shenanigans.

Although its trajectory veers into unexpected places, *The Wailing* never meanders, steering powerfully into its turns and its bias on bias. A shapeshifting beast, the film constantly eschews the expectations of narrative and genre in its exploration of public hysteria and the metamorphic nature of fear.

TRAIN TO BUSAN

부산행

FIRST CLASS HORROR

Seok-woo decides to take his daughter to
Busan for her birthday to see her mother
– but as the train departs, it becomes
apparent that a zombie outbreak is quickly
spreading throughout the country.

2016

Director: Yeon Sang-ho

118 mins

When *Train to Busan* was released in 2016, it was a case of "all aboard!" In Korea, the film caught on quickly, attracting over 11 million viewers. At the time, it was only the 14th film to pass the milestone of 10 million tickets sold, and it broke into the Top 10 highest-grossing Korean films of all time. The hype spread internationally, too, with box office success across Asia, and high-profile cinema releases in the English-speaking world – leading to inevitable discussions about a Hollywood-produced remake.

Its eventual success was far from certain, though. Korean horror had rarely explored the zombie subgenre, at least not with such mainstream appeal. Writer Song Soon-jin at Korean Film Biz Zone points to fringe examples, such as 1981's *A Monstrous Corpse*, 2006's *Dark Forest*, and segments in the anthology films *The Neighbor Zombie* (2010), *Doomsday Book* and *Horror Stories* (both 2012) as precursors, but it is safe to say that *Train to Busan* was exploring new territory in Korean blockbuster cinema.

It was new territory for director Yeon Sang-ho, too. Born on Christmas Day in 1978, Yeon studied Western Painting at Sangmyung University, and pursued a career in animation, inspired by filmmakers such as Satoshi Kon and Hayao Miyazaki, as well as Korean live-action directors Bong Joon-ho, Park Chan-wook and Lee Chang-dong. He made a reputation for himself with dark, provocative

projects that were equally personal and political. His 2011 feature debut, *The King of Pigs*, courted controversy with its horrific depictions of bullying and harassment in the Korean education system. Unsurprisingly, it wasn't a hit, yet it was well-received and screened internationally, including at Directors' Fortnight in Cannes. 2013's *The Fake*, which premiered at the Toronto Film Festival, took aim at organized religion, while *Seoul Station* used zombie-horror metaphors to examine society as a whole.

It was during production of *Seoul Station* that the prospect of a live-action film came up. Yeon credits his backers at the distribution company Next Entertainment World as encouraging him to develop a notion about one of the zombies from *Seoul Station* boarding a high-speed train to Busan into its own feature. Working in live action presented Yeon with the opportunity to reach a much broader audience than his animated work – which received acclaim but rarely earned back their investment. "I wanted to show that trivial incidents, luck, coincidence

Below left and right: Commuter chaos. A busy train proves to be the perfect setting for a claustrophobic horror.

Opposite: Tickets please. Fast-moving and furiously violent, the zombies of *Train to Busan* were something never before seen in blockbuster Korean cinema.

KOREAN ANIMATION

While in the past we have dedicated whole books to Japanese animation, there isn't a Korean animated feature among the 30 films highlighted in this book. The fact is that very few animated films have enjoyed as much success and acclaim, both at home and abroad, as their live-action counterparts, and that is despite a long tradition of animation, from 1967's groundbreaking film *A Story of Hang Gil-dong*, through to recent breakouts such as *Oseam* (pictured) and *My Beautiful Girl, Mari*, which both won the top prize at the Annecy International Animation Film Festival. None of these films received a wide release in the English-speaking world, which is a bitter irony, as there are Korean fingerprints on many household-name animated films and TV series from the past four decades. Companies such as Studio Mir, Sunwoo, Rough Draft, CNK International and AKOM provided

"outsourced" animation work on many landmark productions for foreign networks, ranging from *Batman: The Animated Series*, *X-Men* and *The Legend of Korra*, to *Samurai Jack*, *Steven Universe* and *The Simpsons*, while Seoul's DR Movie has the rare distinction of contributing to two of Studio Ghibli's biggest hits: *Princess Mononoke* and *Spirited Away*.

Above: Rush hour. *Train to Busan*'s everyday railway setting gave it an edge within the clichéd world of zombie horror.

Below: Hungry for more? *Train to Busan* received an animated prequel in the form of 2016's *Seoul Station*.

among others change people from good to bad or vice versa," he told *Korea JoonGang Daily*. "There is no entirely good or bad person. Through such a setting, I hoped it would give a portrait of today's society."

The challenge was to marry this ambitious social commentary with the even more ambitious idea of breaking new ground in a relatively untapped film genre. Yeon was well-versed in Hollywood horror, but for *Train to Busan* he drew specific inspiration from the claustrophobic tension of Paul Greengrass's docudrama thrillers *United 93* (2006) and *Captain Phillips* (2013), and the oppressive atmosphere of downbeat horrors *The Mist* (2007) and *The Road* (2009). This would be mixed with a populist flair that focused on action and emotion, and a reshaping of the zombie archetype for Korean audiences. "Putting a lot of zombie make-up on Koreans doesn't work," he told Screen Daily. "So I focused on movement – using bone-breaking choreography and looking at how we could shoot hordes of zombies and even their shadows inside trains and train stations. Zombies can be stylish and horrifying with the right mise-en-scène."

The results were hugely successful, and a prime example of what academic Keith B. Wagner has described as "glocalization" – a film that remixed international genre tropes to specifically serve a local audience, but which also plays just as well on the world stage. In retrospect, it may seem like a no-brainer, but looking back in 2020 when speaking with the Indian newspaper *The Hindu*, Yeon Sang-ho still considered the response to *Train to Busan*, both at home and abroad, to be nothing short of a miracle.

Below: Class-conscious. For all its blood-thirsty frights, *Train to Busan*'s most monstrous creature is a self-serving salaryman.

FURTHER VIEWING

The world of *Train to Busan* was further sketched out in two stand-alone features: the animated prequel, *Seoul Station*, and the action-packed thriller *Peninsula*, which premiered in Korea amid the Covid-19 pandemic in 2020. Yeon's work since *Train to Busan* has mostly been in the live-action realm, including his distinctive spin on the superhero genre, *Psychokinesis*, and the Netflix series *Hellbound*. That Netflix link is key, as *Train to Busan*'s mix of horror flourishes and class-conscious themes is also apparent in the smash-hit series *Squid Game* (pictured), which features Gong Yoo in a pivotal role in its opening episode. For further family-themed genre spectacle, look back to an early hit by one of Yeon's great influences, Bong Joon-ho, and his 2006 monster movie *The Host*.

Step on board a train in a film and it could take you anywhere, but most of the time, the journey itself is the most important thing. On *The Polar Express*, the destination could be faith; in Studio Ghibli's *Whisper of the Heart*, the route sparks creativity and adventure; and in 1895's *Train Pulling into a Station*, a dramatic stop helps start a whole new art form. Closely confined characters, constant momentum and the rush towards a climactic final destination make trains a vehicle for cinematic spectacle, so add some zombies and you're steaming ahead to a Korean blockbuster smash.

After some thankfully brisk viral exposition, *Train to Busan* introduces us to Seok-woo (Gong Yoo), a divorced workaholic fund manager, who thinks he can buy himself out of any problem – even if that means buying his daughter Su-an a second Nintendo Wii for her birthday, forgetting the one he already got her. What Su-an really wants is her mum, so the emotionally mismatched pair get on the first train out to Busan to see her, but a stowaway with a particularly nasty infection turns the journey into a game of life and death, and an incredibly gory father-daughter bonding session.

As passengers turn into an undead horde, Seok-woo and Su-an join a small gang – like a survivalist *Breakfast Club* – along with a pregnant woman, her husband, an elderly lady separated from her sister, a baseball player and his girlfriend and a homeless man, and they fight their way to the head of the train, in search of safety. Yeon Sang-ho's film isn't particularly groundbreaking in its narrative, but what makes *Train to Busan* so special is how satisfyingly the familiar story plays out. Like Spielberg's *War of the Worlds*, a fractured world and a fractured home are reflected; with a child at its core, the drama of a broken home is an apocalyptic event, one with deadly ramifications. Written by Park Joo-suk, the script is slick and powerful, both in small details and big-hearted beats. A comment made about a scarf keeps viewers eyes on a character's neck, so when the zombies come chomping, there's only one place to look; and

a half-finished song from Su-an at the start of the film is completed at the end, its new verses now carrying the heft of her literal emotional journey.

Underpinning the flesh-eating is a social commentary that's built into the fabric of the train. It's no accident that Seok-woo's a money man, and that his work specifically relates to the origin of the virus; finance is as much a disease as blood-sucking here. The wealthy at the top of the train will do anything to stop the horde getting in, even if it means sacrificing the lower classes for safety. For even more class warfare on rails, make sure you watch Korean master Bong Joon-ho's *Snowpiercer*, a grisly, thrillingly staged post-apocalyptic feature-length metaphor.

There's a thumping physicality to most of the action which manages to give the tale some tactility. Breakout star Ma Dong-seok and his bicep-swelling knockout punches are endlessly entertaining (as is the fact he wears brogues), while the inclusion of a baseball team on the train makes for some splattering fun. All of the bloodshedding is complemented by some gleefully gruesome make-up, but unfortunately the film's lacklustre CGI does break the spell at points; amorphous waves of zombies are thrown around screen, and feel weightless and threatless.

With Covid-19 slightly in the rear-view mirror, *Train to Busan* becomes an even more impactful film to watch. Through smart use of clashing silence and chaos, it invokes the alien fear of being in entirely deserted spaces and then intensely populated spaces with a virus constantly looming, and reminds us of the tribalism to which a polite society is quickly reduced – both of which the pandemic made frighteningly real. Initially a fantasy, now more of a reality than viewers could ever have planned for, the thrilling and heart-breaking *Train to Busan* is a journey that's worth a few return tickets.

Opposite: Peak performance. The international success of *Train to Busan* introduced the world to superstar actors Gong Yoo and Ma Dong-seok.

THE WORLD OF US

우리들

SMALL SCALE

During the summer holidays, 10-year-old Sun makes friends with Jia, who has just moved to town. They soon become best buddies, but that friendship is tested when school starts up again, and Sun becomes the victim of bullying.

2016

Director: Yoon Ga-eun

95 mins

In 2020, following the Oscar success of *Parasite*, Bong Joon-ho was invited to guest-edit an issue of the prestigious British film magazine *Sight and Sound*. In an opening feature, he drew up a list of 20 filmmakers "whose work he believes will be pivotal to the next 20 years". Among the heirs apparent of world cinema – Ari Aster, Mati Diop, Chloé Zhao, Robert Eggers, Ryusuke Hamaguchi – there was only one Korean filmmaker mentioned: Yoon Ga-eun.

Born in 1982, Yoon is one of the leading voices of a new generation of female filmmakers in Korea. After studying History and Religious Studies at Sogang University, Yoon enrolled in the Korea National University of Arts, majoring in Film Directing. She also taught, giving lectures at film clubs for youngsters in Seoul and working for the Korean Film Museum. Working with kids would become a running theme as she started making films of her own – intimate, observational dramas that explore the perspectives, experiences and inner lives of kids and young people.

Below: The floor is drama. With its kid's-eye-view, Yoon Ga-eun crafts intelligent, detailed observations on children's lives.

Opposite top: Poles apart. After initially bonding quickly, Sun and Jia soon have a dramatic falling out.

Opposite bottom: Class and class lead to drama in *The World of Us*, as financial situations and school bullying combine.

FURTHER VIEWING

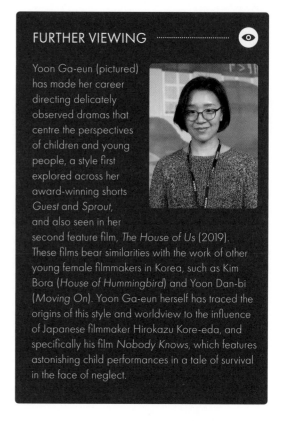

Yoon Ga-eun (pictured) has made her career directing delicately observed dramas that centre the perspectives of children and young people, a style first explored across her award-winning shorts *Guest* and *Sprout*, and also seen in her second feature film, *The House of Us* (2019). These films bear similarities with the work of other young female filmmakers in Korea, such as Kim Bora (*House of Hummingbird*) and Yoon Dan-bi (*Moving On*). Yoon Ga-eun herself has traced the origins of this style and worldview to the influence of Japanese filmmaker Hirokazu Kore-eda, and specifically his film *Nobody Knows*, which features astonishing child performances in a tale of survival in the face of neglect.

Across two short films, she honed her craft. 2011's *Guest* won the Grand Prix at the Clermont-Ferrand International Short Film Festival, while 2013's *Sprout* screened at the Berlin Film Festival and was awarded the Crystal Bear for the Best Short Film by its Children's Jury – a panel of festivalgoers between the ages of 11 and 14. The relationship with Berlin continued with Yoon's feature debut film, *The World of Us*, which received its world premiere there in 2016.

The feature had been developed as part of a programme supported by Korean film distributor CJ Entertainment and the Korea National University of Arts, where Yoon had been mentored by director Lee Chang-dong. When *The World of Us* screened at the Far East Film Festival in Udine, Yoon recalled that the most impactful feedback Lee gave her when working on the film was the simple, yet piercing question: *Do you believe in this story?* "I'm the director of the film, but I need to believe in the story for it to work," she said. "I realized that particularly in a story about children, the moment that it starts to feel staged or fake, the whole thing falls apart."

The feedback chimed with another one of Yoon's key influences: the work of Japanese documentarian-turned-filmmaker Hirokazu Kore-eda, whose powerful everyday dramas feel drawn from real life. "There was a time about a decade ago when I was debating whether I should continue trying to make films," she explained. "Around then I saw Kore-eda Hirokazu's *Nobody Knows*, and it hit me like a shock. It showed me a completely new way to make films, in terms of its approach and perspective. He often depicts very painful and difficult situations, but he presents them with a kind of lightness or simplicity."

Light, simple, painful and real, *The World of Us* opened to acclaim, and Yoon was awarded the Best New Director prize at the Blue Dragon Film Awards, cementing her place as a filmmaker to watch.

Above: Never patronising, treating them like grown-ups, Yoon's film respects the emotional complexity of her young subjects.

Opposite: Written and directed by Yoon Ga-eun. For more sharp, resonant storytelling like *The World of Us*, watch her 2019 film *The House of Us*.

THE WORLD OF US – REVIEW

When children Sun and Jia first meet and stroll around the streets of their hometown, the roads seem to be empty, the paths and shops theirs to pioneer. Briefly, the bustle and stress of adulthood is absent, and in forming a friendship, they form a world of their own; but it's a fragile one. The world of friendship is one that children can shatter and reform in seconds, through barbed words and silent gestures, and it's one that's expertly built by director Yoon Ga-eun.

The World of Us has a seemingly simple focus, the friendship between two young girls, and the adept observations of Sun (Choi Soo-in) and Jia (Seol Hye-in) turn this small-scale story into something universal. Beginning with that most cruel torture of youth, the picking of teams (and inevitable ranking of social hierarchy), Yoon's film never undermines the pains of childhood, respecting the suffering of bullied outsider Sun. She must endure the needling of classmates about her father's drinking, the terror of glares and laughter at her family's lack of wealth, and the ache of loneliness when treading through a school full of social landmines, and her summer friendship with Jia lifts a weight from her. Choi Soo-in's delicate and diverse performance is remarkable: often in silent close-ups, she subtly shifts from anxiety, to joy, to crushing disappointment in seconds, perfectly capturing the elasticity of children's emotion. Although she is first enriched by her friendship with Jia, their union is divided when Jia befriends Sun's bully and

takes on the turncoat role in what becomes an almost Shakespearean tragedy, full of betrayal, shame and even bloodshed.

Given its subject, and its empathetic feel, a large amount of the camerawork in *The World of Us* sits with Sun and Jia at their level, often craning upwards for interactions with adults, the outsiders to their realm. As well as shifting their gaze, the issues of these outsiders shift the girls' relationship, with alcoholism, separation and finance turning from overheard concerns into bullying fodder. The wealth divide between the families of Sun and Jia is a fascinating hinge for drama, with the two children recognizing, but not fully understanding, their diverging lifestyles. In attempting to match the other, Sun steals to buy Jia needlessly expensive items, while the rich Jia shoplifts for the reserved Sun. Their differences are perhaps best illustrated in the film's recurring motif around nail polish. Their friendship is formed around the creation of a home-brewed red floral nail polish, but later the bully Bo-ra (who spurns Jia too) lends her own blue nail polish to Sun, who uses it to cover the red. As the colours combine and eventually peel, a small fragment of red remains, showing that despite their fragmentation, Jia is still a part of Sun. Yoon Ga-eun's film, and its exquisite detailing, are a transporting collage of the beauty and horror of formative youth, which will make viewers yearn for that innocence but be glad they never have to relive it.

A TAXI
DRIVER

택시운전사

FARE WARNING

In 1980, protesting citizens and the Korean military clashed in the city of Gwangju in a horrific series of events that is now referred to as the Gwangju Uprising. This film dramatizes the story of a Seoul cab driver who becomes part of history after escorting a German journalist to Gwangju to cover the incident.

2017

Director: Jang Hoon

137 mins

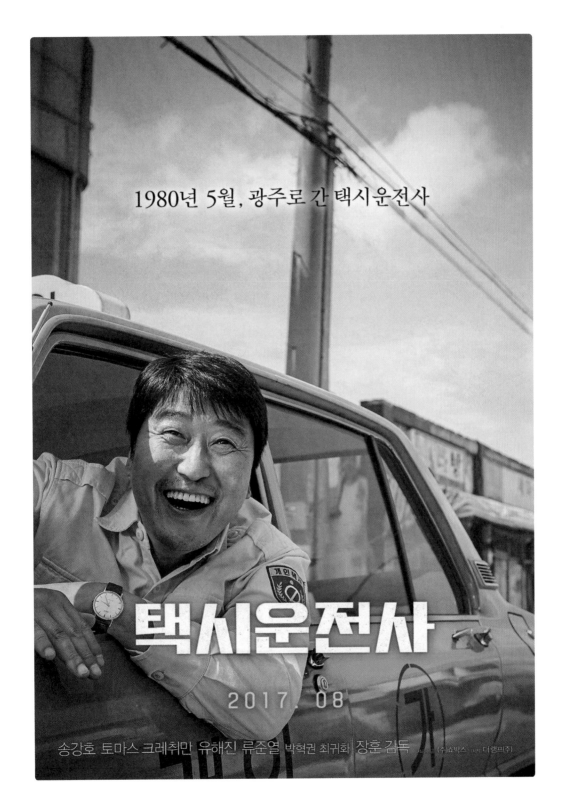

One of the most prominent faces of Korean Cinema on the world stage, actor Song Kang-ho has enjoyed a varied career working with many of the great directors of the day, often forging relationships with figures such as Park Chan-wook, Bong Joon-ho, Kim Jee-woon and Lee Chang-dong on some of their earliest successes and breakthrough hits. He's a director's favourite. When Japanese filmmaker Hirokazu Kore-eda travelled to Korea to make the film *Broker* (2022), a major motivating factor was the opportunity to work with Song. He explained: "What I find appealing about Song Kang-ho is that he has this ability to express two sides, light and dark, lightness and heaviness, good and evil. He can express both of these things. He's the opposite of monotone."

Song himself is self-effacing in interviews, explaining that he was merely in the right place at the right time, perfectly positioned to leave a career in theatre behind to ride on the coat-tails of a new generation of Korean directors. After picking up the Best Actor prize at Cannes for *Broker*, he was asked by *Korea KoongAng Daily* about his popularity with filmmakers, and he replied, "I think it's because I'm ordinary. I'm not handsome, and I am like the guy next door who you see every day, which is what I think makes me approachable, and why I have had the chance to work with so many talented people."

While he's always reluctant to talk about his influences, inspirations or favourite films, there's one actor he likes to highlight: Hollywood legend Steve McQueen, specifically his performance in the 1973 prison epic *Papillon*. He told *The Film Stage*, "I think it's really his nonchalant coolness that I was attracted to growing up, as well as the sort of cynicism he brought to his roles. While it's not true that I became an actor because of McQueen, I will say that he had a considerable influence on my decision to become one."

But while Song works with revered filmmakers of world cinema, he is also a box office draw back home. His biggest hit to date, in terms of ticket sales at least, is *A Taxi Driver*, a historical drama-thriller that uses his grounded, everyman quality to full effect. It was his second collaboration with director Jang Hoon, a one-time protegé of controversial filmmaker Kim Ki-duk, who stepped out of his mentor's shadow to make a series of increasingly successful commercial films. Released in August 2017, *A Taxi Driver* sold over 12 million tickets in just over a month, making it the biggest film of the year, and one of the best-performing films at the Korean box office of all time.

Above, both pictures: Song Kang-ho won his third Blue Dragon Award for Best Actor for his performance as the everyman title character in *A Taxi Driver.*

FURTHER VIEWING

Song Kang-ho is one of Korea's great actors, and has the rare distinction of being one of the members of the so-called "100 Million Viewer Club" alongside fellow actors Hwang Jung-min and Oh Dal-su. He can be found in two further films covered in this book – *Shiri* and *Parasite* – and he also has a brief cameo in *Bad Movie*. See him at the top of his game in *No. 3* (1997), *Joint Security Area* (2000), *Memories of Murder* (2003), *The Host* (2006) and *Secret Sunshine* (2007), or, in one of his personal favourite performances, Kim Jee-woon's *The Foul King* (2000). Many of the most popular Korean films of all time dramatize historical events, such as the spectacular epic war film *The Admiral: Roaring Currents* (2014), set in the 16th century; the spy film *Assassination* (2015), set during the Japanese Occupation; and the nostalgic tearjerker *Ode to My Father* (2014), which looks back at several turbulent decades of the 20th century through the experiences of one ordinary man.

Above: Student union. Journalist Jürgen "Peter" Hinzpeter's work played an important role in furthering the democratization movement in South Korea.

Below: Check point. *A Taxi Driver* dramatizes a horrific event in modern Korean history: the Gwangju Uprising.

Above: It ain't easy being green. In this minimalist teaser poster, the bright green of Mr Kim's taxi stands out against a grey backdrop of foreboding smoke.

A TAXI DRIVER – REVIEW

Forget Travis Bickle. Watch Jang Hoon's gritty, inspiring and surprisingly charming military exposé, and Song Kang-ho's Mr Kim will be the cinematic cabbie that will always come to mind first. A working-class widower, whose beaming smile is like a third headlight on his taxi, Kim is debt-ridden and his greatest pride – even greater than his cab – is his daughter. To help secure his family home, he inadvertently swindles his way into espionage, securing four months' rent in a single journey by taking journalist Jürgen Hinzpeter, known simply as "Peter" (Thomas Kretschmann – Baron Von Strucker in the Marvel series), into the city of Gwangju. There, unknown to Kim, a violent uprising is taking place.

A chipper, sweet man with a hustling streak and a lithe frame and grooving gait, Kim is an unlikely member of a democratic front line, but that's exactly where his journey takes him. From sleek Seoul to explosive, bloody battlegrounds, it's a trip with a cost Kim could never have expected. Showing the kind of everyman heroism that has peppered Tom Hanks' career, Song Kang-ho gradually transforms from cabbie to colonel in a performance that's warm, funny and ferocious, and a perfect foil to his straight-edged passenger.

Having collected Peter in Seoul, with his yellow shirt and lime-green taxi both gleaming, the two deceive their way through checkpoints, share half-translated meals with new allies, and witness, record and

are subjugated to excessive, weaponized brutality wrought by a violent military aiming to stop anti-dictator "commie" students and their supporters. As they descend into the mayhem, the crisp, tropical colours wash out of the film, with smoke, tear gas and a palette of fiery orange placing them in an urban furnace. Jang Hoon's direction of the attacks is stark and physical, with gunshot thumps and buckling bodies providing a seering score, and foggy, silhouetted lurching figures heightening the horror atmosphere.

As the drama goes through the gears, the previously politically unengaged Kim turns, heroically returning to the city after escaping because he "left a customer behind", and in doing so becoming more honourable than the soldiers he once trusted. Once pained more by damage to his car than the wounded student who caused it, he leads a charge to get Peter and his reportage out of the country, culminating in a scene that tugs at the heartstrings when a battalion of taxi drivers arrive like the Riders of Rohan to secure the safe travel of truth. It's a little soapy – Kim and Peter even get their own "rush to the airport" climax – but entirely allowable. Hailing a powerful message, and hiding it in an accessible actioner, Jang Hoon's film is enjoyable, emotional and a journey well worth the fare.

Above: Camera man. Hintzpeter's footage of the events of May 1980 was broadcast around the world.

Left: Gwangju calling. Mr Kim's fare takes him far away from Seoul, and right into the pages of history.

BURNING

버닝

BARN YESTERDAY

Lee Jong-su, a loner who aspires to become a novelist, one day bumps into Shin Hae-mi, a friend from his childhood, who asks him to look after her cat while she goes away on holiday. When she returns, she introduces Jong-su to her new wealthy friend, Ben, and, shortly after, mysteriously disappears.

2018
Director: Lee Chang-dong
148 mins

Author, filmmaker, government minister, teacher, mentor: Lee Chang-dong has worn many hats over the course of his life, and came to his career in film only in middle age, almost by chance. He was born in Daegu in 1954, and his first loves were writing and theatre. As a solitary kid he wrote stories for his own amusement, and saw plays on stage from the age of 10. At university he studied Korean Language Education, and became a high-school teacher while making his start as a novelist, eventually having success with works such as the award-wininng *There is a Lot of Shit in Nokcheon* (which hasn't yet been translated into English).

Then, as he neared 40, he made a change. Speaking at the BFI London Film Festival in 2018, he explained by quoting a Chinese proverb: *Once you're 40, you can no longer be seduced*. In his case, the opposite was true. "On the contrary, when I turned 40, I basically started questioning and having thoughts, queries about the path I was on, about my life. I didn't want to continue down this same path, but try a different path, and that was making films."

Of course, it wasn't quite so simple as that. First, Lee became acquainted with the Korean New Wave director Park Kwang-su while he was making *To the Starry Island* (1993). He was brought on to co-write the screenplay, and ended up serving as assistant director, essentially receiving a crash course in filmmaking from one of the great directors of the period. Lee then returned to write the script for Park's *A Single Spark* (1995), which won Best Film at the Blue Dragon Film Awards and screened in competition at the Berlin Film Festival.

Looking back, Lee credits international film festivals as one of the motivating factors for him to dedicate his life to filmmaking. He told the Korean Film Council, "To me, there is no essential difference between making a film and writing a novel. Both of them are involved in trying to talk to and communicate with an audience." However, films tend to travel in a way that literature seldom does, making it a more enticing proposition for sharing stories with the world.

That impulse is key, because Lee's films have never been blockbusters; instead, they court critical acclaim and win prizes at film festivals around the world. That trend started with his 1997 debut, the gangster thriller *Green Fish*, which won both Best Film and Best Director at the Blue Dragon Film Awards and garnered plaudits from the Vancouver and Rotterdam film festivals. His follow-up, *Peppermint Candy*, opened the Busan International Film Festival and took home Best Film at Korea's other leading awards ceremony, the Grand Bell Awards. Ever since, he has been one of the most lauded and garlanded Korean filmmakers on the world cinema scene: *Oasis* (2002) screened at the Venice Film Festival and netted Lee the Best Director Prize and his star, Moon So-ri, the Marcello

Opposite: Growing suspicious. Setting greenhouses on fire becomes a key plot point in *Burning*, but could the threat of it just be hot air?

Above: Jong-su (Yoo Ah-in) meets Shin Hae-mi (Jeon Jong-seo), sparking the film's twisting narrative.

Below: Lighten up. The enigmatic Ben (Steven Yeun) lights a cigarette, which might not be the only thing he sets on fire.

Mastroianni Award, while *Secret Sunshine* (2007) and *Poetry* (2010) both competed at the Cannes Film Festival, with Jeon Do-yeon winning the Best Actress prize for the former and Lee receiving Best Screenplay for the latter.

When talking about his filmmaking inspirations, Lee is poised between the twin poles of John Cassavetes and Ingmar Bergman, with the legendary independent filmmaker Cassavetes representing freedom and the power that comes from depicting real, human life, and Bergman, the titan of austere world cinema, addressing more artistic, metaphysical considerations. Bergman's films, he told the Korean Film Council, show that cinema "is a medium that can talk about the human soul and about religion, and can save us".

In between film projects, Lee found himself brought into the world of politics when he served as Korea's Minister for Culture and Tourism for a year from 2003 to 2004, but perhaps his more impactful side hustle has been his role as a teacher in directing and screenwriting at the Korea National University of Arts, where he has formed relationships with budding filmmakers, including two covered in this book: July Jung (*A Girl at My Door*) and Yoon Ga-eun (*The World of Us*). An article published in *Sight and Sound* billed as "Ten Tips for Aspiring Filmmakers" gives us a taste of Lee Chang-dong the film professor. One maxim reads: "Always leave your mark. Make audiences remember your name after they watch your film. . . . You need to be always thinking about how

to put your signature on the film, how to prove that the film is yours and no one else's. That might be through your own individual style, your own way of looking at the world or your own sensitivity."

After an eight-year break during which Lee was blacklisted by the Korean government, expectations were high for *Burning* when it premiered in Competition in Cannes in 2018. Lee was inspired to adapt the short story "Barn Burning" by Japanese author Haruki Murakami because of the sense of mystery that Murakami maintained through the story, and the lack of easy resolution, telling the *Hollywood Reporter* that he sought to expand it into "a commentary on the mysteries of the times we are living through, and how ambiguous our lives actually are".

FURTHER VIEWING

Unlike many of his peers and predecessors, whose work can be characterized by wild swings, magpie-like approaches to genre, or prolific work rates, Lee Chang-dong has a contained, cohesive filmography, totalling only six feature films in more than 20 years. It's a frequently gruelling body of work, though, as the director has rarely avoided dark, disturbing and difficult dramatic material, from the tragic lost-youth narrative of *Peppermint Candy*, to *Secret Sunshine*'s heartbreaking study of grief (featuring a powerful performance from Jeon Do-yeon), to the devastating meditation on memory and mortality, *Poetry*. For more cinema drawn from the writing of Haruki Murakami, look for *Norwegian Wood* (2010), *Tony Takitani* (2004), the Oscar-winning epic *Drive My Car* (2021) and the animated anthology *Blind Willow, Sleeping Woman* (2022). Korean-American actor Steven Yeun is on scene-stealing form in *Burning*, and can be found in both lead and supporting roles in the likes of Lee Isaac Chung's *Minari* (2020), Bong Joon-ho's *Okja* (2017) and Jordan Peele's *Nope* (2022).

Opposite top and bottom: Ben, with his modern apartment and wine-soaked nights out with friends, offers a stark contrast to Jong-su's lonely farm life.

Above, top and middle: For more Lee Chang-dong, check out his previous film *Poetry*; and for more Steven Yeun, try *Minari*, which earned a Best Picture Oscar nomination.

Above: Hair raising. Yeun's performance as Ben marked a turn away from his nice guy Glenn in *The Walking Dead*.

"Aren't all protagonists nuts?" Some more than others, few as intriguing as *Burning*'s Jong-su (Yoo Ah-in). This jokey line in Lee Chang-dong's masterpiece is uttered in an early scene in the film, a discussion about stories, sparked by Jong-su who has recenttly graduated with a degree in creative writing. Like a lot of writers, Jong-su spends a lot of time talking about the writing he might do, rather than doing it. Living alone at his family's run-down farm, he is an embittered, lonely man, trying to craft his own life story, looking for direction but finding obsession. Lee's serpentine tale pushes Jong-su from a gormless weed to vigilante, in this gripping, poetic story that's not about a complex hero, but a hero complex.

A million miles (and a bad haircut) away from his fantastically slick and muscular corporate boss in *Veteran*, Yoo Ah-in is Jong-su, who has a chance meeting with childhood friend Shin Hae-mi (a joyous, dynamic Jeon Jong-seo), who asks him to look after her cat while she's away in Africa. Before she leaves, they go to her apartment, the shy cat doesn't appear, and Jong-su and Hae-mi have sex. Jong-su is both starved and distant, kissing like a meat grinder, and staring at a reflection of a tower building on the wall, rather than looking at Hae-mi. He feeds Hae-mi's cat, whose empty bowls suggest it eats and drinks but is never seen. A few weeks later Hae-mi returns, accompanied at the airport by the baby-faced Ben (Steven Yeun, in his post-*The Walking Dead* run of superb supporting roles, also including Bong Joon-ho's *Okja*) – a handsome, rich, charismatic man, whose job is simply, sinisterly, to "play".

A Porsche driver, with a pristine apartment, a large group of friends and a casual confidence not afforded to Jong-su, Ben is both an idol and a nemesis. In the film's centrepiece scene, Ben and Hae-mi arrive unannounced at Jong-su's farm for an evening. A large house, condensely packed with generations of tools and books, making it a prison for Jong-su – and the opposite to Ben's crisp, white flat. Played out in moments of spacious, natural beauty and tight, competitive paranoia, this is where *Burning*'s

plot catches alight. The trio sit in three cheap deckchairs, smoke some marijuana and watch the sun set. Hae-mi starts to dance, her silhouette swirling across a rich purple and yellow sky, before she descends into tears, and bed. Now is when we get the title drop: alone, with the sun gone, Ben tells Jong-su that as a hobby he likes to burn down greenhouses, and that he'll be burning down one close to him very soon. After this point, Hae-mi disappears, and Jong-su starts to investigate Ben's greenhouse burning – or perhaps something even worse.

Structurally, Lee's films are fascinating, unbothered by expectation, and all the more surprising and satisfying for it. *Peppermint Candy* from 1999, a drama about masculinity and trauma, begins with a suicide attempt and is told in chronologically rewinding episodes; 2010's *Poetry* (featuring an incredible performance from the late Yoon Jeong-hee) sets up a narrative shape about Alzheimer's and adult education, before shifting focus to the machinations of a sexual assault-claim payout. *Burning*, at around 90 minutes in, becomes a murder mystery.

In an early scene, Hae-mi shows Jong-su that she's learning mime, holding an invisible tangerine in front of him and through a smile, chewing on it. Like the cat and the greenhouse burning, Jong-su is told about something but never sees it. He perceives stories as truth, without the tangerine slices to prove them. Hae-mi is a bored millennial, stifled creatively, and her disappearance could be simply explained, but Jong-su writes himself into a drama that gives him purpose, and bolsters his masculinity (see also the unfairly maligned, and excellent, *Under the Silver Lake*). Seeing Ben as a Patrick Bateman-style yuppie killer – who even does women's make-up for them, getting to treat them like playthings – and never recognizing his own toxic traits, Jong-su becomes obsessed, his small moment of pleasure with Hae-mi read as an act of duty. Empty, plastic vessels for growth, the greenhouses are a metaphor – a reductive, misogynistic portrait of women by men – and Jong-su strives for justice only to give himself more depth, rather than his subject.

As well as the mystery plot, the miraculous score from Mowg only thrums its deep greeting relatively late into

the film as well. Beginning with long, drawn-out bass notes, accompanied by sparse drum taps, the hypnotizing groove melds with Jong-su's dark enchantment with Hae-mi and Ben perfectly. Twisting and tightening as the story evolves, the low register flips at the height of Jong-su's obsession, with high notes taking the lead, plucked with so much aggression that they sound like they could snap.

Using natural light, Lee shoots Jong-su in bold, but never brash, framing that is both illusive and telling. When he is running in front of a sunset, against a window, or in the dark of his home, his face is not often entirely visible. He believes he is kept in the dark, a disgruntled onlooker; but he's also vague, and unreadable, his bored, confused, slack jaw persistent throughout the film, hidden in the mystery of the

backlight. When he does finally write something, the film's mode switches, shot from outside a window and looking in: a confident Jong-su taps away at a keyboard as a smooth crane shot pulls away, encompassing the city and finally making Jong-su feel part of it. There's an unnatural resoluteness to its composure, which tees up the film's shocking, intensely handheld finale – one that like the question of whether or not there is a cat, or a tangerine, or a burning greenhouse, will be debated with every future viewing. There will be many.

Above: Barn burning. If you're curious about Haruki Murakami's original short story, it can be found in the collection *The Elephant Vanishes*.

HOUSE OF HUMMINGBIRD

벌새

YOUTH TAKES FLIGHT

In 1994, against the backdrop of major events in Korean and world history, Eun-hee, a 14-year-old working-class girl, suffers indifference and abuse at home and at school – until she forms a bond with her Chinese-language tutor.

2018

Director: Kim Bora

138 mins

나는 　　이　　세계가　　궁금했다

1994년, 가장 보편적인 은희로부터

벌새

Much like fellow director Yoon Ga-eun, Kim Bora is a key player in a wave of independent female Korean filmmakers finding acclaim at home and abroad. Her feature debut, *House of Hummingbird*, stands as one of the most lauded and garlanded Korean features of the last decade, travelling around the world for film festivals in Busan, Berlin and London, and picking up scores of awards across the board, including Best New Director and Best Screenplay prizes at Korea's Grand Bell and Blue Dragon awards, respectively.

Kim's route to becoming a filmmaker, too, was something of an international journey. Born in Seoul in 1981, Kim followed an undergraduate course in film at Dongguk University with studies in America, receiving a Masters of Fine Arts in film directing from Columbia University. Her graduate short film, *The Recorder Exam* (2011), received funding from the Korean Film Council, Seoul Film Commission and Kodak Korea, as well as Kickstarter crowdfunding. The finished film won a Directors Guild of America Student Film Award and was a finalist for the Student Academy Awards. "Cinema takes me to another world," she told the website Women and Hollywood. "That world is authentic, real, and welcoming. Cinema doesn't belong to the winner but to the loser/loner. The blissful loser. I like that world."

Yet it would take several years for Kim to make the leap to feature-length filmmaking, telling a story inspired by a nightmare she had while studying in New York. Kim told Women and Hollywood: "The unease I was feeling at grad school was bringing back my past memories and traumas from middle school—a period during which I was most unstable. I realized there was something

going on in that period of my life, and I started to dig into the memories."

Kim spent years piecing together various pots of funding from sources that champion filmmakers who work outside of bigger-budget, commercial Korean cinema. Support came from the Seoul International Women's Film Festival, as well as the Korean Film Council, Seoul Film Commission and the Seongnam Cultural Foundation, with post-production support from the Busan International Film Festival and the Sundance Institute.

These initiatives exist to foster new voices and visions, and Kim is no exception. She cites Chantal Akerman's documentary *Hotel Monterey* (1973) and Edward Yang's Taiwanese epic *Yi Yi* (2000), two films with a strong sense of place and time, as key influences on her work. However, in interviews, she points to art and literature as stronger sources of inspiration: the works of Korean writer O Jeonghui, Hermann Hesse and Stendahl (the latter two of which would be referenced directly in *House of Hummingbird*). "I rarely watch films when I'm writing a screenplay," she told *Notebook*. "I want to get inspired by other mediums." When asked what advice has spurred her on through the years, she pointed to a maxim of Catalan architect Antoni Gaudí: "To do things right, first you need love, then technique."

Opposite top: Leap year. Evocative and profound, *House of Hummingbird* delicately dramatizes a pivotal period of Eun-hee's coming-of-age.

Opposite below: Class act. Young Lead Park Ji-hu gives a heartbreaking performance as the quiet, lonely schoolgirl, Eun-hee.

FURTHER VIEWING

While *House of Hummingbird* leaves us wondering what the future holds for young Eun-hee, we can always look back. The feature is essentially a sequel to Kim Bora's (pictured) sublime short film *The Recorder Exam*, which also features a young girl called Eun-hee struggling for approval from her family while world events play out in the background (in this case, the 1988 Seoul Olympics). Actress Kim Sae-byuk, a standout as Eun-hee's beloved teacher Miss Kim, can also be found in several features from director Hong Sang-soo, including *The Day After*, *Grass* and *The Woman Who Ran*.

Above: Those who can, teach. Ms. Kim Young-ji inspires Eun-hee, and helps her through the trials of teendom.

Below: Table talk. Kim Bora uses family meals as a stage for exploring gender politics in 1990s Korea.

HOUSE OF HUMMINGBIRD – REVIEW

House of Hummingbird is a film full of entrances and exits. Doorways, windows and halls, barriers for entry and openings to truths and new experiences. The impressive scenes either side of these doors are short, detailed and transportive – this is a film of passages.

Remarkable in its scope and its intimacy, *House of Hummingbird* is a beautiful, rewarding work, its snapshot approach to story building a rich sense of time and place, as well as a layered, compelling central character (Eun-hee, played by Park Ji-hu) whose quiet composure carries the film. Like Greta Gerwig's *Lady Bird*, another female-led coming-of-age film, Kim Bora's *House of Hummingbird* is built on compact, quietly powerful scenes that find weight in minor interactions and details, showing how these small moments can shape a life's direction.

"Among all the people you know, how many do you really understand?" This is a question presented to Eun-hee by her beloved tutor Young-ji (a wonderfully soft, but inspiring, supporting turn by Kim Sae-byuk) and it captures the journey that Eun-hee goes on. Dealing with school dramas and fragile friendships, as well as domestic abuse, death and national tragedies, the wallflower-ish young girl, like all adolescents, goes from looking at the world to seeing it.

Although it has more women than men, Eun-hee's home is a male-dominated environment, and Kim's observations drip-feed a fascinating, evolving relationship between her subject and the men surrounding her. A brash, seemingly macho figure, her father only seems to support his son, never Eun-hee, and when caught dancing, he claims to be working on his "tennis swings". Eun-hee's brother, who regularly beats her, only understands the physical; his one moment of tenderness to his sister comes when she has a visible scar. Both angry and pitying, it's a sharp, complex portrait of masculinity, wrapped in a teen girl's story. While her home life is dominated by men, a soothing sequence in a hospital offers an alternative, women-controlled environment. Despite having to have her skull operated on, Eun-hee finds a sanctuary in the female ward; a multigenerational space where

Above: Scarred for life. *House of Hummingbird*'s 1994 setting looks back at the experiences that resonate throughout our lives.

touches aren't violent, giggles and smiles don't have to be hidden and looks of longing can be matched with a kiss. Bathed in white, the almost monastic space is a brief haven, and a confidence spark for Eun-hee.

Throughout the film, characters use plasters, bandages and patches to cover up open cuts, protect scars and relieve deep aches. Ultimately, that's what this film is about: the small nicks, big wounds and lifelong pains that can be formed at childhood, and how people around us can inflict them, and how others, even the most unexpected people, can heal them.

PARASITE

....

기생충

HOME INVASION

When Ki-woo, the son of the poverty-stricken Kim family, is given the opportunity to work as an English tutor for the wealthy Park family, his parents and sister conspire to also land jobs in the household.

2019
—————————————————
Director: Bong Joon-ho
—————————————————
132 mins

행복은 나눌수록 커지잖아요

송강호 이선균 조여정 최우식 박소담 장혜진

제공/배급 CJ엔터테인먼트　제작 (주)바른손이앤에이　15세 이상 관람가

기생충

2019 봉준호 감독 작품 │ 5월 대개봉

"Once you overcome the one-inch-tall barrier of subtitles," director Bong Joon-ho remarked when accepting the Golden Globe Award for Best Foreign Language Film for *Parasite*, "you will be introduced to so many more amazing films." *Parasite* didn't so much overcome that barrier as smash right through it. From its world premiere at the Cannes Film Festival in May 2019, the hype and acclaim grew. It took home the prestigious Palme d'Or, the first Korean film to do so, and ended its campaign run with a historic sweep at the Academy Awards, winning Best International Feature, Best Original Screenplay, Best Director and, the big one, Best Picture.

It was an overnight success decades in the making. Born in 1969 in Daegu, North Gyeongsang, Bong was an introverted child of a family of what has been described as "solitary individuals". His father was an art lecturer at a local university, while his mother was the daughter of Park Taewon, a man of letters and an eminent figure in Korean literature. From a young age, Bong was a fan of comics and a keen doodler, and he would copy illustrations from volumes of the *Britannica Junior Encyclopaedia*. He was also a budding film fan: as a kid, he saw the Korean mecha anime *Robot Taekwon V* (1976) at the cinema, but he had his horizons broadened by watching films on TV and, later, VHS, through which he was introduced to the work of Alfred Hitchcock, John Carpenter and Sam Peckinpah.

Later, he became a keen reader of Korean film magazines such as *Roadshow*, and began collecting VHS tapes bought from the Hwanghak-dong video market, such as the hard-to-find films of Kim Ki-young. At one point, his collection of cassettes both bought and taped totalled 600. A true world cinema fan, Bong counts among his (many) favourite films Martin Scorsese's *Raging Bull* (1980), David Fincher's *Zodiac* (2007), the Coen brothers' *Fargo* (1996), Shohei Imamura's *Vengeance is Mine* (1979), Hou Hsiao-hsien's *A City of Sadness* (1989), Luchino Visconti's *Rocco and His Brothers* (1960) and Ingmar Bergman's *Fanny and Alexander* (1982). In 1994, he enrolled in the Korean Academy of Film Arts, where his studies were supplemented by voracious viewing of his own. He'd recall later that he'd learned "the concept of directing" from Japanese animator Hayao Miyazaki, after spending whole days watching and rewatching the 1970s anime series *Future Boy Conan*.

Bong's graduation project, the three-part satirical short film *Incoherence*, was well received, but his feature debut *Barking Dogs Never Bite*, released in 2000, was overlooked in Korea. "It's an empty, embarrassing feeling," Bong told the Korean Film Council, "like when you're singing in a karaoke room and everyone goes outside to talk

Above: Siblings Ki-woo and Ki-jung sit next to their high-rise toilet to get phone signal. One of many iconic *Parasite* locations.

on their cell phones." The film fared better internationally, though, with screenings at festivals in San Sebastian, Rotterdam, London and Tokyo. In retrospect, Bong believed that *Barking Dogs* proved to be too strange and indulgent for the Korean public, something he rectified with all future projects by marrying his personal sensibilities and inclination towards social themes to more accessible projects, making distinctive, popular genre films in a style that critic Jung Ji-youn has described as "commercial auterism".

His breakthrough came in 2002 with the crime drama *Memories of Murder*, which drew inspiration from a series of unsolved murders that captured the national imagination in the mid-1980s. His first collaboration with actor Song Kang-ho, the film was in some ways a Korean spin on Hollywood thrillers such as *Se7en* (1995) and *The Silence of the Lambs* (1991), but Bong credits Alan Moore and Eddie Campbell's Jack the Ripper graphic novel *From Hell*, a timely gift from critic Tony Rayns, as having the deepest influence on the film, specifically the symbolic use of grisly murders as a reflection of a violent era of history.

2006's *The Host* was an even bigger hit, attracting 13 million viewers, close to one third of the population of the country. Inspired by the shocking revelations that a US military morgue had dumped poisonous chemicals into the Han River,

Top right: Choi Woo-shik's Kim Ki-woo shows off his expertly forged educational certificates.

Right: "It's so metaphorical." Song Kang-Ho's Kim Ki-taek holds the ceremonial rock that seems to "cling" to his family.

KOREA AT THE ACADEMY AWARDS

Parasite's awards success at both the Cannes Film Festival and the Academy Awards (pictured) was a long overdue recognition of the quality of the Korean film industry. At the Oscars, it wasn't just the first Korean film to be nominated for (and win) Best Picture; it was also, remarkably, the first Korean nominee (and winner) for the Best International Film in Academy Award history. Will the impact of *Parasite* change things in the long term? We shall see. But the Best Supporting Actress prize won by Youn Yuh-jung for her performance in Lee Isaac Chung's Korean-American drama *Minari*, following an august career encompassing collaborations with directors including Kim Ki-young and Hong Sang-soo, feels like a good start.

the film was a uniquely Korean big-budget monster movie, with creature design and visual effects from world-class companies such as Wētā Workshop and Industrial Light and Magic alumni The Orphanage. On release, *The Host* was a zeitgeist-grabbing blockbuster, overshadowing Hollywood's franchise behemoths *Mission: Impossible 3*, *X-Men: The Last Stand* and *Superman Returns*.

With his creative ambitions expanding, Bong went abroad to make 2012's *Snowpiercer*, an adaptation of a French sci-fi bande dessinée that boasted an international cast and crew. Another huge hit in Korea, *Snowpiercer*'s release in the English-speaking world was undermined by the ego of Harvey Weinstein, the now-disgraced boss of distributor The Weinstein Company, who demanded cuts to the film that ended up scoring significantly worse with test audiences than Bong's preferred director's cut. The film was eventually released uncut in select US cinemas in 2014, but British audiences would have to wait until 2020 to see the film legally, when the film was quietly released on Amazon Prime Video. Perversely, this was three years behind the release of *Okja*, Bong's anti-capitalist "super pig" satire: another international, multilingual feature, but this time backed by streaming giant Netflix, giving the director his most global audience to date.

After these high-concept, international excursions, *Parasite* plays like something of a homecoming to contemporary Korea as a setting and cultural canvas. Ahead of its premiere in Competition at the Cannes Film Festival in 2019, director Bong requested that journalists refrain from spoiling the film's twists, writing in the press notes: "I believe it is all filmmakers' hope that their audience will experience bated breath at every turn of the story, small and big, that they will be surprised and sucked into the film with burning emotion at every moment."

In his director's statement, he described the film as "a comedy without clowns, a tragedy without villains, all leading to a violent tangle and a headlong plunge down the stairs". True to form, the film played with genre while introducing elements of dark social satire. The title, he granted, might make viewers expect the film to be a monster movie in a similar vein to *The Host*, but instead they were presented with a uniquely thrilling drama he described as an "unstoppably fierce tragicomedy". "It is in parts funny, frightening and sad," he continued. "And if it makes viewers feel like sharing a drink and talking over all the ideas they had while watching it, I'll wish for nothing more." Well, one thing is for sure: the film got a whole lot more than that.

Opposite: About to fold. Early in the film, the Kim family take a job (badly) folding up boxes for a pizza shop.

Above: Rain over me. Bong Joon-ho uses rain to link *Parasite's* two central families, their homes and their wealth.

FURTHER VIEWING

Bong Joon-ho has always acknowledged the strong influence of Kim Ki-young's films on his work, and that's no more evident than in *Parasite*. Bong himself has highlighted that *Parasite's* class-conscious satire, the infiltration of a middle-class family unit, and a central role of a staircase are all informed by Kim's 1960 classic *The Housemaid*. And if *Parasite* was your introduction to the world of director Bong, you are in for a treat. All of his films are worth your time, and as a body of work his filmography is as diverse as it is distinct. From the dark comedy of his offbeat debut *Barking Dogs Never Bite*, to his tonally tricksy serial killer thriller *Memories of Murder* (pictured), the Spielbergian monster movie *The Host*, the unlikely

murder mystery *Mother*, the thoughtful anti-blockbuster future-shock *Snowpiercer* (pictured), and the near-indefinable sci-fi satire *Okja*, the world of Bong Joon-ho is full of surprises and delights.

When Bong Joon-ho was young, he worked as a tutor for a rich family. It was in a luxurious home, fitted with a private sauna, and he thought about introducing his friends to the rich family as well. But the infiltration never happened, he had "great conversations" with his pupil, but crucially they never actually got around to studying, so he was fired after two months. His brief employment may have revealed him to be a bad tutor, but the experience ultimately gave audiences worldwide a cinematic masterclass.

Parasite is many things, including, but not limited to, a tomahawk-sharp satire, a nail-biting home invasion thriller, a slick heist film and a raucous comedy of manners. And in whatever form, at whatever moment, it is always deliriously entertaining. It's the story of the Kim family who reside in a dim, semi-basement apartment that peers just above ground level and who scrape by on piecemeal employment and local, unprotected Wi-Fi accounts. When Ki-woo, the son of the family, is visited by an old friend, he's gifted not only a ceremonious, trophy-like rock ("It's so metaphorical") but the chance to take over his job as tutor to the daughter of the wealthy Park family, and so begins an almighty grift, one that soon becomes a family affair.

The Park house, in contrast to the Kim's almost windowless space, is a sleek but heartless stack of rigid, bragging glass and concrete, high on a hill, designed by the renowned fictional architect Namgoong. The architect in reality is, of course, Bong Joon-ho and his set design team, who created one of 21st-century cinema's most iconic locations, an engineering marvel not just aesthetically but narratively as well. A Rube Goldberg machine inside a hall of mirrors, this remarkable home is full of clues, traps and secrets, built to reflect and distort its inhabitants and its viewers. Once Ki-woo successfully integrates his family, sister and art tutor Ki-jung (Park So-dam, a fantastically natural con woman), mother and housekeeper Chung-sook (Jang Hye-jin, who shows off brilliant comic timing) and father and driver Ki-taek (Bong favourite Song Kang-ho, whose transition from affable calm to boiling rage is the pulse of the film) into Park life, the gleaming home gradually reveals some of its hidden depths, symbolizing societal structure and the poor treatment of its foundations.

As well as imbuing his central location with provoking style, Bong shows his skill throughout the film for bringing meaning and story weight to the objects encountered by his characters. As the takeover turns against them, Ki-woo's rock "clings" to him, its symbolic role malleable, both the promise of a rewarding life and a bludgeoning weapon; motion sensor lights show off the Park home but switch to become a sign of hidden, dark truths; and a dish of Ram-don noodles made with cheap, instant noodles, accessible

to anyone, topped with high-grade, expensive, exclusive cuts of meat, highlights the two families' wealth divide. Even the weather is utilized for superb dramatic effect, with a deluge of rain cascading from the Park house, all the way down town to the Kim's apartment, flooding it. Trickle-down economics visualized perhaps, the potential of flow between classes in reality resulting in the domestic destruction of the less fortunate.

Parasite's script, co-written by Bong and Han Jin-won (assistant director on Okja), is a meticulously crafted work, featuring blink-and-you'll-miss-it hints at future twists (look out for a comment about the Park's original housekeeper's eating habits), sensationally satisfying reveals and a permanent grounding in the class commentary at the film's core. Obsessed with any of his staff "crossing the line" and thinking too much of themselves, Mr Park (Lee Sun-kyun) is oblivious to the Kim family's invasion, but insists that his driver, and even his housekeeper, all have the same smell. Speaking in a Q&A with fellow director Edgar Wright (Shaun of the Dead, Hot Fuzz), Bong explained that the "line is just very artificial, he draws that line for himself, and he wants to ignore the world. Beyond the line he treats the outside world as a ghost. But smell always crosses the line." As much as the wealthy might like to hide away from wider society, it's there, and as much as the Kims might want to assimilate in the camouflage of wealth, it's there – and it's this smell that transports Parasite to its shocking, bloody finale.

A master planner, Bong designed every shot of the film in advance (even using a virtual version of the Park home to strategize his blocking), and worked strictly to his storyboards, without any secondary cameras capturing alternative shots for "coverage". Once pieced together in the editing suite, the rhythm of the story flows wonderfully, offering perfectly balanced moments of contrast, like the gathering of party materials cut against the distribution of flood disaster supplies, as well as sequences of layered momentum, like when the Kim team complete their staff takeover. Soundtracked to Jung Jae-il's grand, classical score, the seven-minute scene is a bravura medley of military manoeuvre and crime caper that reaches a breathless, hilarious climax.

At the time, despite its popularity, Parasite's Oscar win was still a huge surprise. A cross-genre, foreign-language film that challenges capitalist structure but manages to score America's top cultural gong? From today's perspective, that's less surprising: the film showcases storytelling, from both a character and technical level, at its very best. No matter how many times you rewatch it, it always brings the house down.

Opposite: Child's play. Park Da-song's extra-curricular activities, like drawing and playing with a bow and arrow, become key to Parasite's narrative.

Above: Hungry for revolution. Bong Joon-ho uses food, contrasting communal meals with class-skewering noodles for the elite, to season Parasite thematically.

MOVING ON

남매의 여름밤

SUMMER AT GRANDPA'S

After their parents' divorce, two young kids move into their elderly grandfather's house along with their father. Soon, their aunt joins them, bringing three generations of the same family under the same roof.

2019

Director: Yoon Dan-bi

105 mins

Born in Gwangju in 1990, Yoon Dan-bi may be the
youngest filmmaker we've covered in this book, but her
inspiration to become a director sprung from a long-
established source. While she was in high school, Yoon
felt isolated and out of step with her friends who had clear
ambitions for their adult lives – that is, until she watched
Good Morning (1959), the classic family comedy from
Japanese master Yasujirō Ozu. "Even though [Ozu and
I] had never met before," she told Grace Han at Asian
Movie Pulse, "I felt as if he spoke to me personally, that he
knew me deeply. I realised I wanted to make something
like that. A film that resonates with the viewer."

Studies in film at Seoul's Kookmin University followed,
and Yoon enrolled in a graduate film programme at
Dankook University. She directed the short *Fireworks* in
2015, and developed what would become her feature-
film debut as a graduation project. Initially something
of a black comedy, the film was stripped back to its
emotional core. "I think I was unsure and I thought the
film needed a more defined genre," she told the *Korea
Herald*. "That's usually easier to make. But I felt like the
scenario was going nowhere . . . So, leaving just 'family'
in the script, I rewrote the whole thing." Ultimately, she
told the Korean Film Council, the goal was to capture
something sincere, real and lived-in. "I tried to imbue a

Above: Yang Heung-ju and Park Hyeon-yeong as siblings
Byeong-ki and Mi-jeong, navigating their father's care, and
their own personal struggles.

Below: Home is where the hurt is. The family house at the
centre of *Moving On* is full of warmth, but turmoil as well.

Above: Dinner and a show. In a memorable comedic scene, Dong-ju (Park Seung-jun) shows off his dance moves.

Below: Dad joke. Showing his lighter side, Byeong-ki plays a prank on Dong-ju, startling him from his sleep.

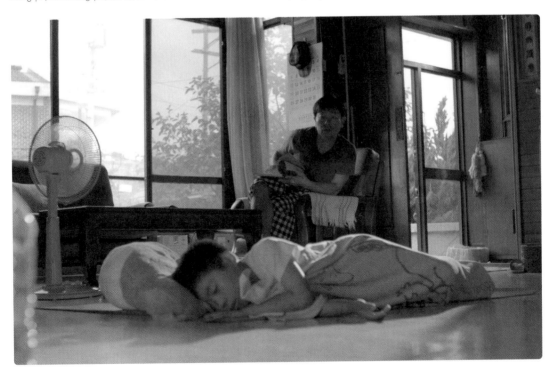

Above: Let the light in. Featuring big, bright windows to light it, director Yoon Dan-bi revels in showing off the details of the central home location.

Below: The garden of few words. Bordered in greenery, the garden provides quiet comfort and sustenance to *Moving On*'s family.

really honest mood. I thought it would be nice if it gave the feeling of visiting someone else's house."

As is the case with the independent side of Korean filmmaking, *Moving On* could only be made with support from various sources, including Dankook University, as well as the Busan International Film Festival and the Korean Film Council. This allowed Yoon, through her production company Onu Films, to capture her vision for a delicate, deeply felt family drama, free of the pressures of commercial cinema.

Moving On received its world premiere at the Busan International Film Festival in October 2019, where it won four prizes, including the Directors Guild of Korea award. From there, it toured around the global festival circuit, attracting acclaim at the Rotterdam Film Festival, where it won the Bright Futures award for Best First Film. Reflecting on her journey, Yoon told Asian Movie Pulse, "Before, there weren't that many independent female filmmakers coming from Korea. Suddenly it feels like there has been a renewed interest in independent Korean cinema. It's pretty empowering; it feels like, yeah, this is actually a viable career path. I can keep making movies."

Below: Love like a sunset. A joyous, innocent moment sees Ok-ju and Dong-ju playing in the street in front of a peach and purple sunset.

FURTHER VIEWING

Moving On, directed by Yoon Dan-bi (pictured), perfectly complements the two other finely crafted family dramas from young women directors covered in this book: Kim Bora's *House of Hummingbird* (2018) and Yoon Ga-eun's *The World of Us* (2016).

Three other noteworthy recent debuts from Korean women filmmakers are *Lucky Chan-sil* (2019), directed by regular Hong Sang-soo collaborator Kim Cho-hee; *Microhabitat* (2017), a character study of a couch surfer slash cultural critique from director Jeon Go-woon; and *Aloners* (2021), a sensitively handled study of social isolation directed, written and edited by Hong Sung-eun.

Observant, wry and delicate, Yoon Dan-bi's film is a sharply drawn and reassuring portrait of a family facing upheaval with grace and quiet fortitude. Like slipping around a velvet rope and into a diorama of glacial, geriatric life, *Moving On*'s teenage protagonist Ok-ju (Choi Jung-un) moves around her grandfather's house – her new summer vacation home – with trepidation and curiosity, fascinated and slightly afraid of the silent, slowly pottering subject at its centre.

Captured in predominantly wide, or mid-length, shots in leisurely long takes, audiences are invited to discover Ok-ju and her family's new world, immersing us in the home and pace of her frail grandfather (Kim Sang-dong). South-facing, large windows help to open the dark house up, Yoon delighting in revealing all its corners and objects in warming sunlight. Other new residents in the wood-panelled rooms are Ok-ju's brother Dong-ju (Seung-jun Park), a precocious boy, attached to and at odds with his subdued adolescent sister; her sparingly employed, reassuringly level-headed single father Byeong-ki (Yang Heung-ju); and later, her soon-to-be divorced, more vivacious aunt Mi-jeong (Park Hyeon-yeong).

Ok-ju's grandfather is a passive but hugely warm presence, who leads a docile life, predominantly inside, being cared for by Byeong-ki and Mi-jeong, but occasionally slipping out to tend to his glorious garden, a bright, green agricultural marvel that reaches above the tall garden walls. The capturing of these domestic rhythms is where Yoon's film is at its finest, especially around food. From the garden harvest to the final plating, characters pluck, chop, and chew throughout the film, finding distraction, grief and reconciliation in the crafting and consumption of their dishes. The precise sounds of slicing, stirring and slurping around a table at points acts as its own dialogue for the melancholy family, with food offering a reprieve to awkward, ominous quiet.

Loose in its plotting, the film occasionally moves out of the central home, Yoon rounding her characters out with slice-of-life scenes. Most enjoyable is

Ok-ju's shiveringly evocative relationship with a boy, all scattered eye contact and fumbling limbs, Choi Jung-un squeezing combustible teenage romance and mortal anxiety together in her superb, simmering performance. Park Seung-jun's Dong-ju is a discovery, too, howling one moment, showing off Pokémon cards at a funeral the next, without being cloyingly innocent or bratty; he's not showy, just naturally performing across the wide-swinging pendulum of a confused child's emotion.

The title is multipurpose, the characters "moving on" from life, from marriage, from grief, from childhood. This is an open film, one with pockets of wisdom and for warming yourself in the sun. "Love is so short. Forgetting is so long" reads the slogan on one of Ok-ju's T-shirts. It will take a short time to fall in love with *Moving On*, and a long time to forget.

Below: It's about the journey, not the destination. Light in plotting, heavy in details, *Moving On* is hard not to be moved by.

Opposite: A gorgeous illustrated poster for the film by the artist Banzisu.

FURTHER READING

Bong Joon-ho: Dissident Cinema, by Karen Han. 2022. Abrams.

Extreme Asia: The Rise of Cult Cinema from the Far East, by Daniel Martin. 2015. Edinburgh University Press.

Film World: Interviews with Cinema's Leading Directors, by Michel Ciment. 2009. Berg Publishers.

Four Rookie Directors, by Choi Eun-young, Kim Young-jin and Jung Ji-youn. 2008. Seoul Selection Co., Ltd.

Hallyu!: The Korean Wave, edited by Rosalie Kim. 2022, V&A Publishing.

Horror to the Extreme: Changing Boundaries in Asian Cinema, edited by Jinhee Choi and Mitsuyo Wada-Marciano. 2009. Hong Kong University Press.

Im Kwon-taek: The Making of a Korean National Cinema, edited by David E. James and Kyung Hyun Kim. 2002. Wayne State University Press.

Korean Film Directors: Bong Joon-ho, by Jung Ji-youn. 2008. Seoul Selection Co., Ltd.

Korean Film Directors: Hong Sangsoo, by Huh Moon-yung. 2007. Seoul Selection Co., Ltd.

Korean Film Directors: Im Kwon-taek, by Chung Sung-ill. 2007. Seoul Selection Co., Ltd.

Korean Film Directors: Jang Sun-woo, by Tony Rayns. 2007. Seoul Selection Co., Ltd.

Korean Film Directors: Kim Ki-young, edited by Kim Hong-joon. 2011. Seoul Selection Co., Ltd

Korean Film Directors: Lee Chang-dong, by Kim Young-jin. 2007. Seoul Selection Co., Ltd.

Korean Film Directors: Park Chan-wook, by Kim Young-jin. 2007. Seoul Selection Co., Ltd.

Korean Film Directors: Ryoo Seung-wan, by Kim Young-jin. 2008. Seoul Selection Co., Ltd.

Korean Film Directors: Shin Sang-ok, by Yi Hyo-in. 2008. Seoul Selection Co., Ltd.

Korean Film Directors: Yim Soon-rye, by Lee Yoo-ran. 2008. Seoul Selection Co., Ltd

Korean Film Directors: Yu Hyun-Mok, by Kim Kyoung-wook. 2008. Seoul Selection Co., Ltd.

Korean Horror Cinema, edited by Alison Peirse and Daniel Martin. 2013. Edinburgh University Press.

New Korean Cinema, edited by Chi-yun Shin and Julian Stringer. 2005. Edinburgh University Press.

New Korean Cinema: Breaking the Waves, by Darcy Paquet. 2009. Wallflower Press.

Rediscovering Korean Cinema, edited by Sangjoon Lee. 2019. University of Michigan Press.

Seoul Searching: Culture and Identity in Contemporary Korean Cinema, edited by Frances Gateward. 2007. State University of New York Press.

Tale of Cinema, by Dennis Lim. 2022. Fireflies Press.

The Cinema of Japan and Korea, edited by Justin Bowyer. 2004. Wallflower.

The Korean Wave: Korean Popular Culture in Global Context, edited by Yasue Kuwahara. 2014. Palgrave Macmillan.

The Remasculinization of Korean Cinema, by Kyung Hyun Kim. 2004. Duke University Press

Who's Who in the Korean Film Industry: Directors. 2008, Korean Film Council.

Women's Cinema, World Cinema: Projecting Contemporary Feminisms, by Patricia White. 2015. Duke University Press.

ACKNOWLEDGEMENTS

This book has been our most ambitious project to date and we couldn't have written it without the help, advice and inspiration of many friends and colleagues.

Thank you to our Ghibliotheque companions Steph Watts and Harold McShiel for the conversations both on mic and off. At our publisher, Welbeck, we're indebted to Joe Cottington, Conor Kilgallon, Giulia Hetherington, Mozidur Rahman and the much-missed Ross Hamilton.

For lending us their expertise and guidance, thank you to Natalie Ng, Daniel Martin, Anton Bitel, David Jenkins, David Cox and Matt Turner. For their work promoting, distributing and contextualizing Korean cinema, we must salute Karen Han, Hayley Scanlon, Hyun Jin Cho, Kate Taylor, Tony Rayns, Jinhee Choi, Darcy Paquet, Dennis Lim, Thomas Flew,

Josh Slater-Williams, Adam Torel at Third Window, Joey Leung at Terracotta Distribution, Jared at Mondo Macabro, the teams at the London Korean Film Festival, the BFI London Film Festival, BFI Southbank, Queer East and London East Asia Film Festival.

Much of this book was written at the British Film Institute's Reuben Library and the Korean Cultural Centre in London. The biggest thank you must go to Eunji Lee of the Korean Cultural Centre and her colleagues at the Korean Film Archive for their generosity and support.

Finally, thank you to Louisa, Mim and Ivo for allowing us to disappear into our respective attic and basement writing dens for yet another adventure into the wide world of cinema.

INDEX

CREDITS

The publishers would like to thank the following for their kind permission to reproduce pictures in this book.

Key: a= above, b= below, c= centre, l = left, r = right

Alamy Stock Photo: AJ Pics 103, 109; Album 66, 99a, 105br, 107a, 114a, 142b, 161a & b, 165, 175a; BFA 176; Cinematic Collection 105a, 107b, 111; Collection Christophel 113b & c, 115, 142a, 159, 160, 162b, 163b; Dom Slike 143a, 175c; Doreen Kennedy/Alamy Live News 114b; Entertainment Pictures 72a, 73, 105c;

Everett Collection 31b, 67, 69, 71a , 86-87a, 88-89, 117, 118, 119b, 121, 123, 125-127, 140r, 145, 153, 154a, 155b, 156, 162a, 163a, 167-168, 170-171, 173;

Landmark Media 163c; Lionel Hahn/Abaca Press 134; Photo 12 12, 98, 100a & bl, 104, 105bl, 106, 112, 113a, 141b, 174, 177a, 178, 179; TCD/Prod DB 7, 8, 16-18a, 18b, 19, 22-25, 50-53, 71b, 72b, 75-77, 78b, 79, 91-92, 92b-95, 99b, 133, 135, 136, 139, 140l, 141, 143b, 177b

Getty Images: Ilgan Sports/Multi-Bits 93a; Jung Yeon-je/AFP 56b, 87b; Kevork Djansezian 175b; K. Y. Cheng/South China Morning Post 62b; Kyodo News Stills 31a; Matt Carr 100br; Matthias Nareyek 119a; MJ Kim 124; PhotoQuest 12b; Theo Wargo/Getty Images for Tribeca Film Festival 169

Courtesy Korean Cultural Centre UK 130b

Courtesy Korean Film Archive 81, 82a

Courtesy and © M-Line Distribution 181-187

Reuters: You Sung-Ho 108; Yuriko Nakao 78a

Courtesy and © Sauve qui peut le court métrage 148a

Courtesy and © Shin Sang-Ok Memorial Foundation 27-30, 33

Courtesy and © Sidus Corporation 59-62a, 63

Shutterstock: Kobal 70, 120, 154b, 155a, 157a & b

Additional copyrights: A24 Films 163c; ATO Inc/Finecut 147, 148b-151;
Barunson E&A/CJ Entertainment 173-175a, 176, 177a, 178, 179;
Beautiful Pictures Co 66; Chungeorahm 99a; CJ Entertainment 64, 67; Di Bonaventura Pictures 99b; Egg Film/Show East 104, 105-107a; Epiphany/Mass Ornament 167-168, 170-171;
Finecut 117; Finecut/Studio Dadashow 142b;
Fox International Productions 8, 133, 135, 136; Grasshopper Film 118, 121;
Gummy Film/CJ Entertainment 129-131; Hwacheon Films 39, 40a, 41; Jeonwonsa Film 117, 118, 119b-121; Kino International 86-87a, 88-89, 163; Korean Film Company 22-25; Kuk Dong – Seki Trading Co 16-18a, 19; The Lamp/Showbox 153-157; Magnolia Pictures 31b; Mago21 Co 141b; Masulpiri/CJ Entertainment 4, 85-87a, 88-89; Masulpiri/BOM Film Productions 97-99a, 100a & bl; Maverick Films/Vertigo Entertainment 78b; Miracin Korea 55-57; Moho Film/CJ Entertainment 105a, 105c; Myung Film 72b, 81, 82a, 83; Nam-a Pictures 43-45a, 46, 47; Neon 173, 176; Oeyun Naegang Co/CJ Entertainment 123, 125-127; Pinehouse Film/Now Films 111-114a, 115, 159-162, 163b, 165; Pinehouse/Uni Korea/Diaphana 163c; Red Peter Films 7, 139-141a, 142a, 143b, 145; Samuel Goldwyn Films 69, 71a;
Samsung 70, 71b, 72a, 73; Sidus Pictures/CJ Entertainment 91-92, 92b-95; Shin Cine Communications 75-77, 79; SnowPiercer/Moho Films/Opus Pictures 177b; Taehung Pictures 50-53; UIP 103, 109; Universal Pictures 107b; Watermelon Pictures/Plus M Entertainment 82b; Well Go USA Entertainment 140r, 145, 153-156, 162a, 167-168, 170-171; Woo-jin Films 18b.

Every effort has been made to acknowledge correctly and contact the source and/or copyright holder of each picture and Welbeck Publishing Group apologizes for any unintentional errors or omissions, which will be corrected in future editions of this book.